The
Common Core
Writing Book

Lessons for a Range of Tasks, Purposes, and Audiences

K–5

Heinemann
DEDICATED TO TEACHERS™

Gretchen Owocki

Heinemann
361 Hanover Street
Portsmouth, NH 03801–3912
www.heinemann.com

Offices and agents throughout the world

The author and publisher wish to thank those who have generously given permission to reprint borrowed material:

Excerpts from *Common Core State Standards* © Copyright 2010. National Governors Association Center for Best Practices and Council of Chief State School Officers. All rights reserved.

Cataloging-in-Publication data is on file at the Library of Congress.
ISBN-13: 978-0-325-04805-5

Editor: Tobey Antao
Production: Vicki Kasabian
Cover and interior designs: Monica Ann Crigler
Cover photograph: Rolf Bruderer/Blend Images/Getty Images
Typesetter: Kim Arney
Manufacturing: Steve Bernier

Printed in the United States of America on acid-free paper
17 16 15 14 13 EBM 1 2 3 4 5

For David Owocki and our splendid little Emilia

CONTENTS

Acknowledgments   xiii

Overview   xv

Some Options   xv

The Places We Could Go   xvi

Organization of the Book   xvii

The Types of Instruction   xix

DEMONSTRATION   xx

COLLABORATIVE ENGAGEMENT   xx

INDEPENDENT APPLICATION   xx

TEXT TYPES AND PURPOSES: Anchor 1 1

Grade-Level Standards for Writing: Anchor 1   1

Decision Tree for Writing Anchor 1   2

Demonstration   3

OVERARCHING LESSON   4

MINILESSONS 19

Generating Meaningful Topics 19

Stating an Opinion 19

"Here's what *I* thought" .20

"In *my* opinion" 20

Using words to express an opinion 21

Outlining Reasons for an Opinion 22

Creating an Organizational Structure 23

Use a planning map 23

Use sticky notes 23

Use subtitles 23

Crafting a Strong Introduction 24

Learn from professional authors 24

Try different opening techniques 24

Providing a Sense of Closure 25

Learn from professional authors 26

Try different closure techniques 26

Collaborative Engagement   27

Analyzing and Evaluating Writing Samples from the Classroom .27

Analyzing and Evaluating Mentor Text 28

Conferring with the Teacher 29

Conferring with Peers .30

Independent Application   31

Personal Responses to Literature 31

Book Reviews 31

Literary Essays 32

Persuasive Letters 32

Persuasive Essays 33

Blogs 33

Persuasive Video or Photo Documentaries 34

Advertisements 34

TEXT TYPES AND PURPOSES: Anchor 2 36

Grade-Level Standards for Writing: Anchor 2   36

Decision Tree for Writing Anchor 2   37

Demonstration   38

OVERARCHING LESSON   38

MINILESSONS 54

Finding a Meaningful Topic 54

Organizing and Managing a Piece 54

  Using assigned categories or headings 55

  Developing categories 55

  Using a planning map 55

  Sharpening the focus 56

Developing the Content 56

  Elaboration 57

  Stretching a statement .57

  Freewriting or freedrawing 57

  Reading 58

Using Illustrations and Other Media 58

Crafting a Title 59

  Rationalizing title preferences 59

  Practice with titles 59

  Considering titles across genres 59

Crafting a Strong Introduction. 59

    Learn from professional authors 60

    Try different opening techniques 60

Providing a Sense of Closure. 60

    Learn from professional authors 60

    Try different closure techniques 60

Collaborative Engagement   64

**Analyzing and Evaluating Writing Samples
from the Classroom**. 64

Analyzing and Evaluating Mentor Text. 65

Conferring with the Teacher. 65

Conferring with Peers. .65

Independent Application   67

All-About Books. 67

How-to Pieces. 67

Informational Articles. .67

Research and Lab Reports. 67

Informational Web Pages. 68

Oral Presentations. 68

Informational Documentaries. 70

    Photo documentaries 70

    Video documentaries 71

Newsletters and Memos. 71

TEXT TYPES AND PURPOSES: Anchor 3. 72

Grade-Level Standards for Writing: Anchor 3   72

Decision Tree for Writing Anchor 3   73

Demonstration   74

    OVERARCHING LESSON   75

    MINILESSONS 88

Finding a Topic 88

Creating an Event Sequence 89

    Sketch the sequence 89

    Jot notes about the sequence 89

    Use a narrative map 89

    Use sticky notes. 89

Establishing the "Situation" 90

Using Description 91

    Detailing a person, place, or thing. 91

    Elaborating an event. .92

    Using sensory details .92

    Showing, not telling. .92

    Drawing from word lists 92

    Rewording 93

    Learning from professional authors 93

Using Dialogue 94

    Learning from professional authors 94

    Trying out speech bubbles 94

    Practicing with a painting 94

    Practicing with a picture book 95

    Weaving in dialogue .95

    Scripting comic strips 95

    Filling in a story. 95

    Using dialogue tags .95

Using Words and Phrases to Signal Event Order. .96

    Making the process explicit 96

    Learning from other students 96

    Learning from professional authors 97

    Practice with sequencing. 97

Pacing 97

    Weighting the ideas .97

    Exploring pacing techniques. 98

Crafting a Narrative Text Title 99

    Playing with three 99

    Rationalizing a text title 99

    Rationalizing title preferences 99

    Using graphic design. 99

Providing a Sense of Closure 99

    Learning from professional authors 99

    Trying different closure techniques 100

Collaborative Engagement   101

**Analyzing and Evaluating Writing Samples
from the Classroom**. 101

Analyzing and Evaluating Mentor Text. 101

Conferring with the Teacher 103

Conferring with Peers. 103

Independent Application   105

Personal Narrative 105

Memoir 105

Testimonio 106

Oral History 106

Biography 106

Narrative Fiction 107

PRODUCTION AND DISTRIBUTION OF WRITING: Anchor 4 . . .109

Grade-Level Standards for Writing: Anchor 4   109

Decision Tree for Writing Anchor 4   110

Demonstration   111

OVERARCHING LESSON   112

MINILESSONS: CLARITY AND COHERENCE 116

Rereading 116

Staying on Topic 116

Including Everything Important 117

Weeding Out the Unimportant 118

Attending to Sentence Order 118

Use every other line 119

Number the sentences .119

Attending to Sentence Content 119

Sentence dividing 119

Sentence combining 119

Paragraphing 120

Identifying the uses of a paragraph 120

Paragraph locating 121

Paragraph dividing 121

**MINILESSONS: APPROPRIATENESS TO TASK,
PURPOSE, AND AUDIENCE** 122

Choosing Appropriate Content 122

Choosing Appropriate Formats and Media 123

Attending to Voice 124

Reading and listening .124

Studying different voices on the same topic 127

Adding voice 127

Removing voice 127
Practice matching voice with task,
purpose, and audience. 127

**Merging Attention to Role, Audience,
Format, and Topic (RAFT)** 128

Collaborative Engagement   130

**Analyzing and Evaluating Writing Samples
from the Classroom** 130

Conferring with the Teacher 130

Conferring with Peers 131

Independent Application   133

PRODUCTION AND DISTRIBUTION OF WRITING: Anchor 5 . . .134

Grade-Level Standards for Writing: Anchor 5   134

Decision Tree for Writing Anchor 5   135

Demonstration   136

OVERARCHING LESSON   137

MINILESSONS 143

Quick Editing Minilessons 143

Using an Editing Checklist 143

Using Copy Editing Symbols 144

**Encouraging the Circling
of Suspicious Spellings** 144

Studying Correct or Incorrect Usage 145

Using an Editing Circle 145

Playing with Punctuation 146

Opportunities for Rereading 146

Collaborative Engagement   147

**Analyzing and Evaluating Writing Samples
from the Classroom** 147

Analyzing and Evaluating Mentor Text 147

Conferring with the Teacher 148

Conferring with Peers .149

Independent Application   151

PRODUCTION AND DISTRIBUTION OF WRITING: Anchor 6 . . . 152

Grade-Level Standards for Writing: Anchor 6   152

Demonstration   153

STRUCTURING THE LESSONS   154

Whole Class 154

Small Group 154

Producing and Publishing Writing   156

Word Processors 156

Publishers 156

Web-Based Composing Tools 156

Apps for Composing 159

Digitally Created Visuals 160

INTERACTING AND COLLABORATING WITH OTHERS   161

Document Projectors 161

Interactive Whiteboards 161

Web-Based Document Sharing Platforms 161

Student-Created Websites and Web Pages 162

Blogs 162

Social Media and Networking Sites 162

Independent Application 163

RESEARCH TO BUILD AND PRESENT KNOWLEDGE: Anchor 7 164

Grade-Level Standards for Writing: Anchor 7   164

Planning and Demonstration   165

PLANNING RESEARCH OPPORTUNITIES   166

OVERARCHING LESSON   168

Collaborative and Independent Application   171

RESEARCH TO BUILD AND PRESENT KNOWLEDGE: Anchor 8 172

Grade-Level Standards for Writing: Anchor 8   172

Demonstration   173
USING NOTE-TAKING FORMS   174
MARKING PRINT SOURCES   178
MARKING DIGITAL SOURCES   179

Independent Application   181

RESEARCH TO BUILD AND PRESENT KNOWLEDGE: Anchor 9 182

Grade-Level Standards for Writing: Anchor 9   182

Demonstration   183
OVERARCHING LESSON   184

Collaborative Engagement   191
Analyze and Evaluate Writing Samples
from the Classroom 191
Conferring with the Teacher 191
Conferring with Peers 191

Independent Application   193

RANGE OF WRITING: Anchor 10 194

Grade-Level Standards for Writing: Anchor 10   194

Supporting Routine and Wide Writing   195

Appendix   197

Works Cited   217

Acknowledgments

I wish to express my gratitude to the people who have influenced and supported the writing of this book:

- **Legendary children Mil and Rea** for having such heart as writers. Your article reviews, action letters, and journal entries, and your pieces on fairies, fouettés, flies, skeletons, swimming, cats, cartwheels, and how to get hurt have reminded me daily of *why* I do what I do.

- **Colleague Melissa Kaczmarek** for always being at her screen while I am at mine; ever ready to read sections, contribute ideas, and muse together over changes in the field.

- **Teachers Tia Hahn and Lamar Holley** for sharing ideas of one sort or another.

- **Colleague Anne Tapp** for checking over some of the vocabulary.

- **Dean Susie Emond** for believing in this content and supporting this work.

- **The graduate students at Saginaw Valley State University** for tackling all the hard issues that come their way and for providing so many examples of teaching at its best.

- **Everyone at Heinemann.** There is nothing more encouraging than knowing that while I am at work on my end, the engine out east is also humming along. Kate Montgomery, Eric Chalek, Sarah Fournier, and Vicki Kasabian, thank you for your bright ideas and for always knowing your stuff. And who IS this new editor I have? Don't know what she looks like; don't know what she sounds like; but DO know that she works with grace, humor, high standards, and an incredibly discerning eye. Thank you, Tobey Antao. You are everything I had hoped you would be.

Overview

Everywhere we turn, conversations about the Common Core State Standards (CCSS) are at hand. National conferences are providing sessions; state departments are holding meetings; books and journal articles are being published; blogs are buzzing; websites are being developed; and teachers are sharing ideas. For the first time ever, schools across the United States are using a common set of literacy standards to guide assessment and instruction—and educators and school leaders are grappling with the implications.

Many have examined their existing practices in light of the new standards and are making curricular and instructional overhauls in the areas they feel need their attention first. Others are wondering whether it is enough to simply be aware of the new standards—and for the most part to continue with or gently tweak existing practices. Others, admittedly, have never paid much attention to state standards and are wondering if there is a reason to pay attention now. Some educators are concerned that new standards—regardless of how they are used—may not have much positive impact on student learning; after all, good teaching is good teaching regardless of the standards we have. And there are others who fear that because standards are quite often linked with standardized testing, teachers will feel compelled to place an emphasis on test preparation rather than on fostering broadly meaningful literacy. Clearly, the issues are complex.

Some Options

Within such complexity, we could approach the adoption of the standards in a number of ways. We could sit tight until we have more information about how the new assessments will play out, or until we know exactly what our state offices will be recommending regarding curriculum development. But this suggests that the important professional knowledge lies outside the school, and that educators should wait to make changes even though they may already have some of their own powerful ideas ruminating. And, in fact, many educators across the country have already been busy making decisions about the new standards and how to use them as a starting point to make instruction better: more engaging, more challenging, and more in tune with their students' needs.

So another possible response is to get focused and quickly start teaching and assessing in light of the new standards. Schools could scramble to provide professional learning experiences for teachers: right now, right away. They could make quick switches to new types of lesson planning and new report cards, and individual teachers could start searching for new ideas to try out and share. But such efforts don't necessarily involve a system for nurturing a balanced or manageable approach to improvement that is based on solid evidence, planning, and discussion.

Yet another option is for educators to come together and start looking for curricular programs that advertise "comprehensive" and "research-based" ways to meet the new standards. There has been an asymptotic rise in programs touting a strong alignment with the CCSS. But we are teaching in an era in which research evidence has confirmed that the *teaching*—not the program—is the most important variable affecting student achievement (Cunningham and Allington 2011). Research has not identified any single approach to teaching writing that is going to be effective with every learner (Writing Now 2008).

The Places We Could Go

At the crossroads created by the Common Core State Standards, there are many paths we could take. Because effective teaching does not emerge from a set of standards, a mandate, a state office, or a manual, we must avoid paths that cast educators as secondary decision makers or that offer quick solutions or static packages. Effective teaching results from the skillful weaving of curriculum, carefully selected instructional practices, and thoughtful responses to children's daily activity. Therefore, we must use this crossroads as an opportunity for educators to focus on *teaching*—and on *improving teaching*—to meet this new set of standards that has raised the expectations for student learning higher than ever.

School and district teams can start by implementing the most promising practices known to date, and this book is designed to support this effort. The instrumental practices you will find on the following pages have been used effectively by many teachers; here they are altered and redesigned with special attention to the CCSS. Of course, we can't just implement these practices without also watching our students. Along with teaching practices you will find support for observing students and collecting data to improve and fine-tune your instruction. It is recommended that planned observation be initiated with each new lesson taught; with each new day; with each new unit or theme. Effective teaching involves taking note of children's knowledge and responses to instruction and actively responding in light of both.

As we shape the new system and work within it, we must take care to not lose sight of *meaningful* teaching and learning. In working toward the new standards, kids are going to be doing hard things. Kindergarten and first-grade students are to compose opinion pieces; second- and third-grade students are to use technology (including keyboarding) to produce and publish writing; fourth- and fifth-grade students are to research and write about content-area topics—and they are expected to use grade-level reading material to do so. Aiming for students to perform well with such tasks doesn't mean that we must abandon our work toward a meaningful curriculum. Within the new system, teachers who have managed to "get it right" with writing can still allow students to write for authentic reasons; they can still support their exploration of multiple genres, when the time is right to explore these genres; they can still offer students choices; and they can still arrange for them to begin to shape through their writing meaningful legacies as human beings. Children can still write for reasons that matter. These goals are not inconsistent with the goals of the Common Core State Standards—and in fact having them in place will strengthen our work with the standards.

But as we consider the new standards, the time *is* ripe for improvement. Not all teachers are effective teachers of writing. Many have a very limited writing curriculum, as evidenced by kindergarten and first-grade students writing mostly on worksheets or mostly to develop letter recognition and phonics knowledge; second- and third-grade students writing only in journals or only for ten minutes each morning; fourth- and fifth-grade students writing only from personal experience or mostly from assigned prompts that are reflective of items appearing on the state test. Not all teachers have a plan in place for observing students and shaping and differentiating their instruction based on actual classroom observations. Not all teachers have a system in place for collaborating with other teachers and staying in tune with new findings in the field. There is work to be done. This book can help.

Organization of the Book

The goal of *The Common Core Writing Book* is to support K–5 teachers as they provide differentiated instruction in relation to the ten Common Core writing standards. (See Table A.) The book is organized into ten sections, one for each standard. The ten *anchor* standards provide overarching goals for K–12 students, while more specific sets of standards (outlined at the beginning of each section of the book) define the specific competencies K–5 students are expected to develop by each year's end.

In general, students are expected to work with their grade-level standards. This is with the understanding that some students will need extra support mastering certain competencies from earlier grades before they can demonstrate full competency with their own grade-level standards. In turn, others may be ready to move forward and explore concepts beyond the range recommended. When planning instruction it is helpful to look below and

Table A

Category	Anchor Standards for *Writing*	Page
Text Types and Purposes	**1.** Write arguments to support claims in an analysis of substantive topics or texts, using valid reasoning and relevant and sufficient evidence.	**1**
	2. Write informative/explanatory texts to examine and convey complex ideas and information clearly and accurately through the effective selection, organization, and analysis of content.	**36**
	3. Write narratives to develop real or imagined experiences or events using effective technique, well-chosen details, and well-structured event sequences.	**72**
Production and Distribution of Writing	**4.** Produce clear and coherent writing in which the development, organization, and style are appropriate to task, purpose, and audience. (Begins in grade 3.)	**109**
	5. Develop and strengthen writing as needed by planning, revising, editing, rewriting, or trying a new approach.	**134**
	6. Use technology, including the Internet, to produce and publish writing and to interact and collaborate with others.	**152**
Research to Build and Present Knowledge	**7.** Conduct short as well as more sustained research projects based on focused questions, demonstrating understanding of the subject under investigation.	**164**
	8. Gather relevant information from multiple print and digital sources, assess the credibility and accuracy of each source, and integrate the information while avoiding plagiarism.	**172**
	9. Draw evidence from literary or informational texts to support analysis, reflection, and research. (Begins in grade 4.)	**182**
Range of Writing	**10.** Write routinely over extended time frames (time for research, reflection, and revision) and shorter time frames (a single sitting or a day or two) for a range of discipline-specific tasks, purposes, and audiences. (Begins in grade 3.)	**194**

beyond your grade level to understand the full context for what students are being asked to do.

Any time we think about instruction in writing, we are in a natural position to also think about instruction in *language*, and the Common Core Language standards provide some focus. Of particular importance to writing, the first three Language standards address (1) *grammar and usage*; (2) *punctuation, capitalization, and spelling*; and (3) *understanding how language functions in different contexts*. Therefore, ideas for embedding language instruction into writing instruction are included in this book, with a special focus on the first three Language standards. (See Table B.)

Table B

Category	Anchor Standards for *Language*	
Conventions of Standard English	1. Demonstrate command of the conventions of standard English grammar and usage when writing or speaking. 2. Demonstrate command of the conventions of standard English capitalization, punctuation, and spelling when writing.	These standards are addressed in the lessons for Writing Anchor 5.
Knowledge of Language	3. Apply knowledge of language to understand how language functions in different contexts, to make effective choices for meaning or style, and to comprehend more fully when reading or listening.	This standard is addressed in the lessons for Writing Anchors 1, 2, 3, 4, and 5.
Vocabulary Acquisition and Use	4. Determine or clarify the meaning of unknown and multiple-meaning words and phrases by using context clues, analyzing meaningful word parts, and consulting general and specialized reference materials as appropriate. 5. Demonstrate understanding of figurative language, word relationships, and nuances in word meanings. 6. Acquire and use accurately a range of general academic and domain-specific words and phrases sufficient for reading, writing, speaking, and listening at the college and career readiness level; demonstrate independence in gathering vocabulary knowledge when encountering an unknown term important to comprehension or expression.	These standards are addressed in *The Common Core Lesson Book* (Owocki 2012). See both the *Literature* and *Informational Text* sections.

The Types of Instruction

Rather than providing a curriculum with suggested maps and timelines, *The Common Core Writing Book* provides you with a comprehensive framework of strategies for enhancing a curriculum that is already in place, or for developing your own. For each standard/skill area, three types of experience are suggested:

- Demonstration

- Collaborative Engagement

- Independent Application

This layout makes it possible to implement an approach of demonstrating various techniques and strategies for writing, giving students opportunities to write and try out the strategies in a supportive environment, and ultimately encouraging a gradual takeover of responsibility and control by the students.

Suggestions for differentiating and intensifying instruction are offered in the form of minilessons and teacher conferencing—both of which take shape in response to observations of students and their writing.

Demonstration

Teacher guidance is high during the *demonstration* phase. The teacher uses an *overarching lesson* to lay out general expectations regarding what to include in a piece of writing, how to develop a piece of writing, or how to conduct research and record information. As students write and try out new ideas, techniques, strategies, and genres, *minilessons* are chosen based on observations of student writing and observations of students as they write. The overarching lessons and the minilessons can be used with small groups (including intervention-based groups) or the whole class, throughout the year. They should be selected and adapted based on the particular strengths and needs demonstrated in your classroom.

Collaborative Engagement

Guidance is still high in the *collaborative engagement* phase, but with more allowance and encouragement for students to take responsibility for their own learning and discussion. In the collaborative engagement phase, students engage in group activity and conversation related to the concepts taught in the demonstration phase. Key experiences include students collaboratively evaluating samples of writing, studying particular elements of craft found in mentor texts, conferring with peers, and conferring with the teacher.

Independent Application

In the *independent application* phase, students are given time to write for a variety of tasks, purposes, and audiences supporting their participation in a range of discipline-specific writing experiences. Suggestions are provided for engaging students in writing in different genres, conducting research projects, reporting information, and drawing information from texts. Regularly during the independent application phase, you may cycle back to demonstration and collaborative engagement to provide further guidance.

TEXT TYPES AND PURPOSES

ANCHOR 1

English Language Arts Standards: Writing ANCHOR 1

Writing Anchor 1: Write arguments to support claims in an analysis of substantive topics or texts, using valid reasoning and relevant and sufficient evidence.

Kindergarten	First	Second	Third	Fourth	Fifth
Use a combination of drawing, dictating, and writing to compose opinion pieces in which they tell a reader the topic or the name of the book they are writing about and state an opinion or preference about the topic or book (e.g., *My favorite book is . . .*).	Write opinion pieces in which they introduce the topic or name of the book they are writing about, state an opinion, supply a reason for the opinion, and provide some sense of closure.	Write opinion pieces in which they introduce the topic or book they are writing about, state an opinion, supply reasons that support the opinion, use linking words (e.g., *because, and, also*) to connect opinion and reasons, and provide a concluding statement or section.	Write opinion pieces on topics or texts, supporting a point of view with reasons. **a.** Introduce the topic or text they are writing about, state an opinion, and create an organizational structure that lists reasons. **b.** Provide reasons that support the opinion. **c.** Use linking words and phrases (e.g., *because, therefore, since, for example*) to connect opinion and reasons. **d.** Provide a concluding statement or section.	Write opinion pieces on topics or texts, supporting a point of view with reasons and information. **a.** Introduce a topic or text clearly, state an opinion, and create an organizational structure in which related ideas are grouped to support the writer's purpose. **b.** Provide reasons that are supported by facts and details. **c.** Link opinion and reasons using words and phrases (e.g., *for instance, in order to, in addition*). **d.** Provide a concluding statement or section related to the opinion presented.	Write opinion pieces on topics or texts, supporting a point of view with reasons and information. **a.** Introduce a topic or text clearly, state an opinion, and create an organizational structure in which ideas are logically grouped to support the writer's purpose. **b.** Provide logically ordered reasons that are supported by facts and details. **c.** Link opinion and reasons using words, phrases, and clauses (e.g., *consequently, specifically*). **d.** Provide a concluding statement or section related to the opinion presented.

Decision Tree for **Writing** ANCHOR 1

> ## Is now a good time for focused instruction in relation to Writing Anchor 1?
>
> Anchor 1 requires that students *write opinion pieces focused on texts or topics*. When your students have reason to express their opinions through writing, it is recommended that you implement three types of instruction:
>
> | **Demonstration** | **Collaborative Engagement** | **Independent Application** |
> |:---:|:---:|:---:|
> | Page 3 | Page 27 | Page 31 |
>
> An initial overarching demonstration occurs first, followed by a formative assessment. After analyzing the assessment data, you can use the information below to decide what to teach next and whether this instruction is needed for the whole class or small groups.

Minilessons

After the overarching lesson and formative assessment, choose from the following based on student needs:

- Generating Meaningful Topics (page 19)
- Stating an Opinion (page 19)
- Outlining Reasons for an Opinion (page 22)
- Creating an Organizational Structure (page 23)
- Crafting a Strong Introduction (page 24)
- Providing a Sense of Closure (page 25)

Collaborative Engagement

Use the following experiences to encourage deeper consideration of key writing concepts:

- Analyzing and Evaluating Writing Samples from the Classroom (page 27)
- Analyzing and Evaluating Mentor Text (page 28)
- Conferring with the Teacher (page 29)
- Conferring with Peers (page 30)

Independent Application

When you have students ready to explore new genres of opinion writing, consider the following:

- Personal Responses to Literature (page 31)
- Book Reviews (page 31)
- Literary Essays (page 32)
- Persuasive Letters (page 32)
- Persuasive Essays (page 33)
- Blogs (page 33)
- Persuasive Video or Photo Documentaries (page 34)
- Advertisements (page 34)

You may cycle back through these applications throughout the year, addressing techniques for revising and editing as described in Sections 4 and 5; bringing in technology as described in Section 6; and teaching research skills as described in Sections 7–9.

Demonstration

Anchor 1 requires that students write *opinion pieces* focused on texts or topics. An opinion piece may range from a brief statement of preference supported by an illustration to an elaborated point of view supported by a carefully organized set of reasons and information. Opinion pieces can be composed in varied formats, such as personal responses to literature, book reviews, persuasive letters, persuasive essays, literary essays, advertisements, and blogs. They may be written in first or third person.

Learning to write a high-quality opinion piece can enrich learning across content areas. With such skill, students can develop substance for conversations about literature and art; they can deliberate meaningfully about topics in science and health; and they can begin to take a stance on social issues that are important to them. In fact, instruction in opinion writing develops some of the most critical skills necessary for active participation in a democratic society. "If young people grow up learning to participate in logical, reasoned, evidenced-based arguments, this will mean that they are given a voice. Our democracy is dependent on an educated, concerned citizenry, exercising the right to be heard" (Calkins, Ehrenworth, and Lehman 2012, 136).

To get your students started on opinion writing, it is recommended that you provide an overarching lesson highlighting the key elements to include. The lesson that follows features a set of tools for teaching a flexible beginning structure for an opinion piece as well as an assessment tool to help you identify key next steps for instruction. The lesson may be implemented as many times as needed, and may be used any time a new genre or format for opinion writing is introduced.

Overarching Lesson

To prepare for this lesson, have in mind a format (such as a letter or a book review) and a topic related to your curriculum or to a recent event or discussion in your classroom. You will be demonstrating how to organize and write an opinion piece appropriate to your grade level, and then providing time and support for students to write their own.

1. **Purpose**

   - Discuss the general purpose of an opinion piece. Help students understand that opinion pieces are written to share a viewpoint, or to "make a case." We might write a book review with the goal of convincing everyone in the class that the text is funny and worth reading; we might write a note to a parent to make a case for allowing a stray cat to come inside; we might write an editorial for the community pleading for an end to littering.

   - Tell students that you will be showing them some important things to include in an opinion piece. Explain your chosen topic and format and let them know that they will be writing a piece using the same format.

2. **Expectations.** Briefly show students the expectations for opinion writing at your grade level. Use an enlarged *checklist* (Figure 1–2) or a *map* that includes your required grade-level components (Figures 1–3 to 1–5). Just quickly point out what is typically included in such a piece so that students have a sense of the text type before they write. Emphasize structure, but only to the point that it gives students ideas for creating substantive *content*. Too much emphasis on structure can lead students to plugging in ideas and words just to be "done" rather than allowing them to get a feel for putting a heartfelt opinion on paper.

3. **Demonstration**

   - Use either the checklist or the map as a guide to show students how you play around with the organization of and lay out your ideas. Either *tell* students what you plan to include, showing where on the page you would place your ideas and any illustrations, or *draft the text as they observe.*

   - Tell students that the parts you are showing them should be used in their own writing because they help to build a convincing case. *Note for using the maps:* Students may use a map as their *only draft* or as their *plan*, composing the more formal piece after all the ideas have been laid out on the plan. Before asking students to create narrative from material laid out on a map, demonstrate the process, emphasizing concepts such as paragraphing and linking words.

4. **Student Writing**

- Guide students to brainstorm a specific direction for their opinion pieces. (*My favorite book/painting in the display is _____ because. . . . This character/historical figure is brave because. . . . We should have a rule that _____ because. . . .*). Figure 1–1 offers a set of open-ended prompts to help you get started. Early on, encourage a focus on familiar topics so that students can put their energy into including the key structural elements. Later, they can tackle content that may require new reading or referencing sources.

- Arrange adequate time for students to write. Let them know that this is a "show what you know" piece that you will use to inform your next steps in instruction.

For English Learners

Although English learners (ELs) may go through a period in which they don't say much in class, we can rest assured that they have opinions just like the rest. Work with ELs in light of their specific topics to ensure they get a strong start. For example, you might:

- Work together to develop the language for the opinion statement and then send the student off to write or draw the rest of the piece, checking in as necessary.
- Work together to construct the opinion statement as well as the language for one of the "reasons," and then send the student off to develop that reason before checking in again.
- Work together to construct the opinion statement and a starter sentence for each reason and then send the student off to complete the piece independently.

You may have other students you want to pull in for step-by-step support as well. But as a rule of thumb, avoid *always* placing ELs with students who are expressing difficulty with the content or not achieving at grade level. Students learning a new language only sometimes have the same needs as students who are not meeting grade-level expectations.

FOR ALL STUDENTS

When guiding students to develop opinion pieces, be aware that personal, familial, social, and cultural influences are always at play in children's lives and will impact the ways in which they proceed. For example, some students are generally less open to expressing personal opinions than others; some may not want to express an opinion that might disrupt a sense of harmony with others; some families may believe it is inappropriate for children to express opinions about what parents should do or how they should behave; and some students may be uncomfortable expressing opinions in relation to political issues or the actions of political leaders.

5. **Assessment.** When you have collected an opinion piece from all of your students, evaluate the writing to determine the extent to which students are meeting your grade-level expectations for Anchor 1. Using a class record (Figures 1–6 to 1–11) will offer an overview of what the class needs and will show individual students' growth from a pre- to a postassessment.

Using Assessment to Inform Instruction

To continue your instruction after the initial assessment, first decide whether students will move on to a new piece or revise/continue to work with the current piece. As you provide minilessons, students need to have specific pieces in mind to which they can apply the concepts you are teaching. If the class record shows that most students could use instruction in a particular area, it is advisable to keep the class together for the minilessons. If the record shows varied needs, then provide a mix of minilessons, pulling students in to work with you depending on the needs they have demonstrated. The decision tree on page 2 can help you to set your course.

Figure 1–1

Prompts to Support Opinion Writing

- **Write to show your opinion about a topic we have studied in science.** (Examples: *forest conservation, recycling.*)

- **Write to show your opinion about a topic we have studied in social studies.** (Examples: *equal rights, an issue on a current ballot.*)

- **Write to show your opinion about a topic we have recently discussed.** (Examples: *becoming bilingual, standing up to bullying.*)

- **Write to show your opinion about a text or piece of art you have read/ listened to/viewed.** (Examples: *argue that a text should be read by everyone in fifth grade; argue for a theme.*)

- **Write to show your opinion about a character or real person in a text.** (Examples: *argue that someone is heroic or brave.*)

- **Write to show your opinion about a person you know or a person in the news.** (Examples: *write to share the opinion that someone is a good friend or excellent family member; that someone is making a positive impact on the world; that someone would make a good president or leader in the school.*)

- **Write to show your opinion about something important to you.** (Examples: *argue that pets are important; argue that we learn important things by watching television or playing video games.*)

- **Write to show your opinion about something that you enjoy.** (Examples: *argue that a certain book, game, video game, or electronic device has a value such as being interesting, fun, educational, thought-provoking, or funny.*)

- **Write to show your opinion about a product or place.** (Examples: *review a toy; argue for a best restaurant or best place to visit.*)

- **Write to show your opinion about something you want to change.** (Examples: *argue for less homework or a different kind of homework; argue for the reinstatement of afternoon recess.*)

- **Write to show your opinion about a way to make the world a better place.** (Examples: *argue that animals should not be used in circuses; argue that plastic shopping bags should be banned.*)

- **Write to show your opinion about a specific assigned concept or idea.** (Examples: *We have excellent/poor reading material in our classroom; timed tests are a good/poor tool for learning; rewards are important/not necessary to encourage reading; we should/should not always wear a helmet when biking or skateboarding.*)

CHECKLIST OF EXPECTATIONS FOR WRITING ANCHOR 1

Kindergarten

❏ Tells the topic or title.

❏ States opinion or preference.

Grade 1

❏ Introduces the topic or title.

❏ States an opinion.

❏ Supplies a reason for the opinion.

❏ Provides closure.

Grade 2

❏ Introduces the topic or text.

❏ States an opinion.

❏ Supplies reasons that support the opinion.

❏ Uses linking words.

❏ Provides a conclusion.

Grade 3

❏ Introduces the topic or text.

❏ States an opinion.

❏ Creates a structure that lists reasons.

❏ Provides reasons that support the opinion.

❏ Uses linking words and phrases.

❏ Provides a conclusion.

Grade 4

❏ Introduces the topic or text.

❏ States an opinion.

❏ Creates a structure for grouping related ideas.

❏ Provides reasons supported by facts and details.

❏ Uses linking words and phrases.

❏ Provides a conclusion.

Grade 5

❏ Introduces the topic or text.

❏ States an opinion.

❏ Creates a structure that logically groups ideas.

❏ Provides logically ordered reasons supported by facts and details.

❏ Uses linking words and phrases.

❏ Provides a conclusion.

Figure 1–3

Opinion Map: Kindergarten

Name: _____ Date: _____

Title: _____

Text or Topic

Opinion or Preference

Figure 1–4

Opinion Map: Grade 1

Name: _____ Date: _____

Introduction to
Text or Topic

Opinion

Reason

Closure

Figure 1–5

Opinion Map: Grades 2–5

Name: _____ Date: _____

Introduction to Text or Topic

Opinion Statement

Reason

Reason

Supporting Facts and Details
(You may use sticky notes here.)

Supporting Facts and Details
(You may use sticky notes here.)

(continues)

Opinion Map: Grades 2–5

Reason

Supporting Facts and Details
(You may use sticky notes here.)

Reason

Supporting Facts and Details
(You may use sticky notes here.)

Conclusion

Figure 1–6

Class Record for Opinion Writing: Kindergarten

Student Names	Grade-Level Expectations			
	Tells the topic or title.		States opinion or preference.	
	Date	Date	Date	Date

0 = Not Present　　　　**1 = Could Use Development**　　　　**2 = Developed**

Figure 1–7

Class Record for Opinion Writing: Grade 1

Student Names	Grade-Level Expectations							
	Introduces the topic or title.		States an opinion.		Supplies a reason for the opinion.		Provides a sense of closure.	
	Date	Date	Date	Date	Date	Date	Date	Date

0 = Not Present   **1 = Could Use Development**   **2 = Developed**

Figure 1–8

Class Record for Opinion Writing: Grade 2

Student Names	Grade-Level Expectations									
	Introduces the topic or text.		States an opinion.		Supplies reasons that support the opinion.		Uses linking words.		Provides a conclusion.	
	Date	Date	Date	Date	Date	Date	Date	Date	Date	Date

0 = Not Present   1 = Could Use Development   2 = Developed

Class Record for Opinion Writing: Grade 3

Student Names	Grade-Level Expectations											
	Introduces the topic or text.		States an opinion.		Creates a structure that lists reasons.		Provides reasons that support the opinion.		Uses linking words and phrases.		Provides a conclusion.	
	Date	Date	Date	Date	Date	Date	Date	Date	Date	Date	Date	Date

0 = Not Present   1 = Could Use Development   2 = Developed

Figure 1–10

Class Record for Opinion Writing: Grade 4

Student Names	Grade-Level Expectations											
	Introduces the topic or text.		States an opinion.		Creates a structure for grouping related ideas.		Provides reasons supported by facts and details.		Uses linking words and phrases.		Provides a conclusion related to the opinion.	
	Date	Date	Date	Date	Date	Date	Date	Date	Date	Date	Date	Date

0 = Not Present   1 = Could Use Development   2 = Developed

Class Record for Opinion Writing: Grade 5

Student Names	Grade-Level Expectations											
	Introduces the topic or text.		States an opinion.		Creates a structure that logically groups ideas.		Provides logically ordered reasons supported by facts and details.		Uses linking words, phrases, and clauses.		Provides a conclusion related to the opinion.	
	Date	Date	Date	Date	Date	Date	Date	Date	Date	Date	Date	Date

0 = Not Present   1 = Could Use Development   2 = Developed

Minilessons

Through your initial observations and assessments, you will note some specific areas in which you want to provide additional instruction—either for certain students or the whole class. The minilessons may be implemented with small groups or the whole class.

Generating Meaningful Topics

Topics for opinion writing may come from the texts children are reading, the curricula they are studying, or from their life experiences. While you may occasionally assign some topics, allowing students to choose their own will yield the most engaged writing and therefore the best opportunities for teaching—provided that students choose meaningfully. The following procedures will help to support students in generating topics they care about.

1. Secure a writer's notebook that you can use for demonstrations with the whole class. Show students how to reserve a page for recording topic ideas related to opinion writing. As they observe, start a list of possible topics for your own writing. Your topic should represent the general topic area you want your students to pursue. (See Figure 1–1.) (If you are working with kindergarten students, you may sketch your ideas.)

2. Provide a writer's notebook for each student. Give students time to work with a partner or team to record at least three of their own ideas, staying within the parameters you have set. (Kindergarten students may sketch their ideas.) Encourage students to ask, "Is this something I care about? Do I want to convince others about this topic?" *Note:* As an alternative to having students create their own idea lists, develop a list of possibilities with the whole class. Students could then choose topics from the list or generate their own similar possibilities.

Stating an Opinion

When talking with students or assessing their opinion pieces, it may become clear that the concept of *opinion* or *stating an opinion* is unclear. For example, one first-grade student's opinion statement about a favorite book was written as follows: "Traction Man had a gen sut" (*green suit*). While the student *did* think this event was funny (an opinion), he had not yet mastered the concept of *stating* an opinion. In another classroom, a kindergarten teacher tried to solve this issue with "Tell *why* you think your chosen book was interesting." This led to responses such as Koko wotd a cnt!!!!!! (*Koko wanted a kitten*). Again, an interesting part of the text involved the fact that a gorilla wanted a kitten, but the pieces sound more like retellings or descriptions than opinions. These children are doing good thinking and are ready to stretch their writing further. To help your students learn how to move forward with stating opinions about texts or topics, consider the following minilessons.

"HERE'S WHAT *I* THOUGHT." Read aloud a carefully selected text. Choose something hilarious, terribly boring, gross, or surprising—something that will inspire students to express their opinions. Encourage each student to tell or write what they thought about the text, beginning the statement with "Here's what *I* thought," and using language to show it's an opinion. "I thought this book was interesting because Koko wanted a kitten." Emphasize that opinions may differ because they are personal viewpoints rather than something that is necessarily "true" or "fact."

"IN *MY* OPINION." Plan a firsthand experience in which students compare two objects or materials. For example, you might give teams a set of different bouncing balls or toy cars, two types of Play-Doh, or two different types of jump rope or Frisbee. The task of the team is to play, compare, and come up with an opinion about which materials are best to play with.

1. Tell students that you are going to team them up with two or three other students and give them some time to play. Let them know that they have a job to do. They will be given certain objects/toys to use, and they are to report back regarding which materials are "better" or "work better" *in their opinions*.

2. Give the students time to play. Monitor their activity in a way that helps them to talk about the materials and convene on an opinion about which is better or best. For example, "In our opinion, the heavy jump ropes are easier to use" or "In our opinion, the home-made Play-Doh is best for sculpting."

3. Bring the groups back together to report on their findings. Act as scribe, helping students to articulate their findings in the form of opinion statements.

    Kindergarten: Students may then copy their statement and either write or draw a picture that helps to show the reasons for their opinion.

    Grades 1–5: You may either continue as scribe to record student reasons for their opinions or send students off in teams to record their reasons. Use the opportunity to highlight the use of linking words and phrases (such as *because, also, therefore*, and *since*) to connect reasons and opinions. Beginning in grade 2, students are expected to use linking words in their opinion pieces. This experience can serve as preparation for students to compose their own pieces on the toys/materials explored.

USING WORDS TO EXPRESS AN OPINION. Exploring the specific vocabulary associated with opinion writing will help students learn to express opinions and develop understandings about the genre. This lesson is focused on expressing opinions about *literature*, but it can also be focused on expressing opinions about people, characters, topics, and issues.

1. Gather three or four texts that are familiar to the class and coach students to express their opinions about them. "In my opinion, this book was engaging," "In my opinion, this book was weird," or "I thought it was funny when. . . ." Pull out the most important words (*engaging, weird, funny*) and record them on chart paper. You may wish to create columns on the chart so that in subsequent minilessons students can generate words for expressing opinions about other things, such as characters or current issues. Figure 1–12 shows an example of the type of words that might be included on a chart you create with your students over the course of a few lessons.

Figure 1–12

Using Words to Express an Opinion		
Literature	**Characters/People**	**Topics/Issues**
funny	important	best/worst
makes me think	caring	most/least
weird	principled	negative/positive
page-turner	knowledgeable	healthy/unhealthy
hard to understand	brave	safe/dangerous
has an important lesson	smart	harmful/helpful
quick-paced	kind	fair/unfair
engaging	funny	important/unimportant
sad	imaginative	sensible/senseless

2. Give students an additional text to discuss in a group. Familiar texts work best. Students jot down some describing words that express their opinions about it. Add the words to the chart.

3. Encourage students to think about and add to the opinion words as they are shaping their ideas for opinion pieces. Younger students who are using mostly drawing to express their opinions should be encouraged to use the words to label their drawings.

Outlining Reasons for an Opinion

A strong opinion is backed by *reasons* supported with facts and details. The Common Core standards call for kindergarten and first-grade students to state an opinion or preference with a reason. In grade 2 and beyond, students are expected to use more than one reason. To support students in learning to argue with a set of reasons walk them through a visual outlining process.

1. Select a topic that is meaningful to the group and generate an opinion statement related to it. For example, within a thematic study of recycling, you might use, "All families should consider using compost containers."

2. Put the opinion statement at the top of a page to form the beginning of a hierarchical visual (see below). Or use sticky notes so that you can move the ideas around. Avoid one-paragraph-per-reason formulas, as this may limit creativity and/or force bad paragraphing.

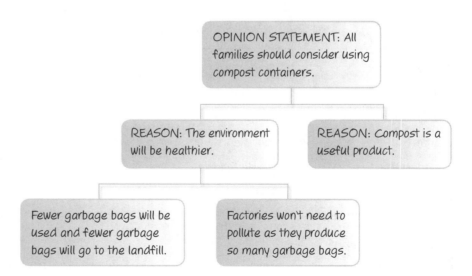

3. Work with the students to generate reasons for the opinion, listing each reason in its own box below the opinion statement. List any facts and details below the reasons. Use the opportunity to discuss the use of linking words such as *because*, *also*, *for example*, and *in addition* to create clarity and flow.

4. Encourage students to use a visual map to lay out the reasons behind their opinions as they prepare for or organize a piece.

Creating an Organizational Structure

Children's opinion pieces often end up with a lot of good ideas in a mixed-up order, or with a lot of ideas, only some of which relate directly to the topic at hand. This can stem in part from writing without planning. To support student development of a logical flow in their opinion pieces, demonstrate any of the following planning processes, and then provide opportunities for students to try the process themselves. IMPORTANT: As students move from planning to composing, be sure to emphasize the incorporation of linking words to ensure a coherent piece.

USE A PLANNING MAP. Show how you can use a planning map to organize your ideas before writing. Figures 1–3, 1–4, and 1–5 are designed for this purpose. For grades 3–5, you may also wish to demonstrate the use of an interactive map from the web. ReadWriteThink offers an excellent tool for opinion writing: www.readwritethink.org/files/resources/interactives/persuasion_map/.

USE STICKY NOTES. Show how you can use sticky notes to lay out an opinion piece. Write your opinion statement on one sticky note and then write reasons for your opinion on additional notes (one each). Line up the reasons beneath the opinion. As appropriate, use additional notes to add facts and details for each reason, tucking the notes under the reason. Write a conclusion and place that beneath the row of reasons.

USE SUBTITLES. As students gain experience categorizing their ideas or reasons (as with the sticky notes and planning maps above) show them how to create a subhead for each reason and possibly for the opinion statement and conclusion. Eventually, students can be encouraged to drop the maps or sticky notes as a scaffold and move straight to using subheads as they draft. Looking at professionally published literature will help them understand how to meaningfully name their subheads. For example, in *Protecting*

Endangered Species, instead of using "Reason 1," "Reason 2," "Reason 3," and "Reason 4," author Felicity Brooks *names* the reasons for protecting species: *Food for the future, Fuel from the forest, Marvelous medicines*, and *Enjoying our world.* As students begin to use subtitles in their own writing, you can begin to use student-created pieces to show good subtitle work.

Crafting a Strong Introduction

Crafting a strong introduction is often one of the final tasks for the writer of an opinion piece. (It helps to have a sense of what the whole piece looks like before attempting the introduction.) Many students easily grasp the importance of introducing a piece. It just makes sense to let the reader know up front what it is going to be about. The challenge is to move beyond something formulaic. While a formulaic introduction *can* serve the function of setting the stage for a piece, it rarely has the draw of a more richly crafted introduction. A strong introduction to an opinion piece hooks the reader and starts building openness toward the case being made.

LEARN FROM PROFESSIONAL AUTHORS. Show students the openings to a small set of opinion pieces or statements and ask what makes them strong or not strong. (Figure 1–16 provides a recommended set of texts.)

TRY DIFFERENT OPENING TECHNIQUES. Compile a list of three or four techniques for opening an opinion statement. (You can add to the list over time.) Start with a direct or formulaic option so that students can compare it with other techniques. Post the list with a set of examples related to a piece you are currently using for demonstration, discussing the techniques you have listed (see Figure 1–13). For whatever piece they are working on, assign students to try out two or three different openings and then work with a peer or team to help determine a favorite.

Figure 1–13

Techniques for Opening an Opinion Statement

- **Direct statement**: This essay is about smoking. I think people should avoid smoking.

- **Personal connection**: My friend Gordon was starting to cough more often. The doctor said it was because he had been smoking for 22 years. Being friends with Gordon, I have an opinion about smoking. I think people should avoid it.

- **"Draw-in" question**: Do you know someone who smokes? Do you ever worry about this person's health? Smoking can be hazardous to health and kids should think twice before starting.

- **Fact-based question**: Did you know that smoking causes about 20 percent of our country's deaths each year? I think it's important to avoid smoking.

- **Fact or detail**: Smoking causes about 20 percent of our country's deaths each year. In my opinion, people should avoid smoking.

- **Quotation**: "Smoking is the most preventable cause of death in the United States" (http://pbskids.org/itsmylife/body/smoking/article2.html). I think people should avoid smoking.

- **Analogy**: A cigarette is like a little piece of poison. I think people should avoid smoking.

- **Snapshot**: On Saturday, my friend Gordon held his cigarettes over the trash can in the parking lot and cut them in half with scissors. I think this was a pretty good idea.

- **Observation from the senses**: Gordon's car already smells better. He hasn't smoked in his car for a whole month! Aside from a fresh car, there are lots of reasons to avoid smoking.

Providing a Sense of Closure

The end of an opinion piece is just as important as the introduction. An ending should provide a sense of closure, and help the reader to consider the key point one more time, perhaps through a new lens. Yet students often fall into a formulaic ending that doesn't pack much power. They close with statements such as "And those were three reasons we thought you should read this article" or "And that's why I think littering is a bad choice." The following strategies may be implemented to help your students explore different closure techniques.

Techniques for Closure

- *Reinforcement:* Rephrase your introductory statement about the case you want to make. Focus on reinforcing rather than repeating.

- *Quotation:* Find a quotation that backs your opinion. You might need to write something before or after the quotation so that it makes sense to the reader.

- *Short story:* End with a very short personal story related to the opinion.

- *Question:* End with a question that will get readers to think about their own opinions on the matter.

- *Humor:* End with a humorous statement.

- *Image:* End with a captioned photo or illustration that supports your opinion.

LEARN FROM PROFESSIONAL AUTHORS. Show students the endings to a small set of opinion pieces/statements and ask what makes them strong or not strong. (Figure 1–16 provides a recommended set of texts.)

TRY DIFFERENT CLOSURE TECHNIQUES. Review a set of closure techniques, using your own writing as an example. Assign students to try two or three different techniques in their own pieces and then work with a partner or team to select a favorite. (Figure 1–14 provides some example techniques.)

Collaborative Engagement

To enhance their understanding of key opinion-writing concepts, arrange for students to engage in collaborative analysis and evaluation experiences, peer conferences, and teacher conferences.

Analyzing and Evaluating Writing Samples from the Classroom

After teaching students about the key elements of an opinion piece (as per grade-level standards), give groups a sample of student writing (or use teacher writing if you don't yet have a student sample) and ask them to analyze it in light of particular criteria. When working with Anchor 1, select from questions such as those featured in Figure 1–15. After groups meet you can bring the whole class together for a follow-up discussion.

Figure 1–15

Questions for Analyzing and Evaluating Opinion Pieces

Grades K–5

- Can you tell how the author feels about the topic? How?
- How is the opinion stated or shown?
- What reasons are given or shown for the opinion? Are there other reasons or details the author could include?
- What key words and phrases are used to express the opinion?

Grades 1–5

- How does the author introduce the piece? Does the introduction begin to draw the reader toward the opinion? How? If not, what other ideas could the author try?
- What reasons does the author use to help convince? Who would be drawn toward these reasons?
- How did the author close the piece? If the closing doesn't move you, what other ideas could the author try?

Grades 2–5

- How is this piece organized?
- What linking words are used?

Analyzing and Evaluating Mentor Text

Using a specific set of questions (as in Figure 1–15) to analyze the craft within professionally published literature or websites can open students to new ideas to consider for their own writing. Figure 1–16 offers a starter list of texts that includes letters, book reviews, movie reviews, and stories.

1. Show students how to reserve a section of a writing notebook to record great ideas or language from mentor texts. They need not record all ideas encountered, but should instead focus on their favorites.

Figure 1–16

Mentor Texts for Opinion Writing

Children's Literature with Opinions and Arguments

- *Click, Clack, Moo: Cows that Type* (Doreen Cronin)
- *Dear Mrs. LaRue: Letters from Obedience School* (Mark Teague)
- *Ike for Mayor: Letters from the Campaign* (Mark Teague)
- *Otto Runs for President* (Rosemary Wells)
- *Duck for President* (Doreen Cronin)
- *Vote for Me!* (Ben Clanton)
- *The True Story of the 3 Little Pigs* (Jon Scieszka)
- *The Perfect Pet* (Margie Palatini)
- *I Wanna New Room* (Karen Orloff)
- *Those Shoes* (Maribeth Boelts)
- *All the Places to Love* (Patricia MacLachlan)
- *Hey, Little Ant!* (Phillip Hoose)

Websites with Reviews

www.commonsensemedia.org

www.kidsfirst.org

www.amazon.com

www.bestcatbreeds.com

http://animal.discovery.com/breed-selector/dog-breeds.html

http://animal.discovery.com/breedselector/catselectorindex.do

http://www.toyportfolio.com/

2. After students read, view, or listen to a text, set them up in groups and give each a copy of the text, directing them to a specific section as appropriate. Assign the groups to work through one to three guiding questions, such as those featured in Figure 1–15. You can differentiate by having different groups work with different questions or texts. In preparation for responding back to the larger group or class, they can jot their ideas in their notebooks.

3. Arrange time for the groups to report their findings and observations.

Conferring with the Teacher

Conferences are important for all student writers. Conference time may be used to listen to students talk and help them articulate their opinions, to teach a specific strategy, or for a quick follow-up to see how newly learned strategies are being incorporated. As a rule of thumb, keep the focus on *teaching the writer* rather than *perfecting the piece*. It can be tempting to help the student create a flawless piece, but it is generally more beneficial to focus on one key concept or strategy that the student can carefully consider and internalize.

When conferring in relation to Anchor 1, keep your focus on Anchor 1 objectives. Organizing the conference with a predictable set of prompts and questions can help students know what to expect and be ready to show you their thinking. See Figure 1–17.

Figure 1–17

Conference Routine

- **Open the conversation.** *How are things going with this piece? Show me how you built your opinion. Is there something you need help with?*

- **Identify notable strengths.** *This part of your drawing catches my eye because. . . . Your introduction draws me in because. . . . Your reason for this opinion is well developed because. . . . This conclusion works so well because. . . .*

- **Identify one teaching point.** *What do you think you revise or do next from here? Can you show me how you will start? I have one thing I want you to develop and I'm going to help you get started.*

- **Send the student away with something manageable to develop.** *Let's get you started on this and then next time we meet we can talk about how it's going.*

Conferring with Peers

Children can be very capable and responsible responders to their peers' writing, especially when they are given some starting expectations for their conversations. After they have some experience conferring with you, coach them to work in peer conferences through any of the processes featured in Figure 1–18.

Figure 1–18

Peer Conference Plans

- Ask the author to tell you the opinion being built and then to read the piece with you. Then tell the author how you feel about the opinion.

- Tell the author what you feel is a big strength and offer one suggestion. Help the author get started on the suggestion.

- Write a response to your peer on a sticky note. Tell one strength and offer one suggestion.

- Ask the author, "What opinion are you building?" Then, "Show me your reasons." Ask the author to tell you more details about one part of the picture or one part of the writing. Help the author get started on adding details about that part, if needed.

- Together with the author, look at our opinion writing checklist (see Figure 1–2) and find all the key parts. Are all the parts present?

- Together with the author, ask: Does this whole piece make sense? Help the author get started on fixing any parts that do not make sense.

Independent Application

The independent application section offers suggestions for helping students move into different genres of opinion writing. You may cycle back through these applications throughout the year, addressing techniques for revising and editing as described in Sections 4 and 5, bringing in technology as described in Section 6, and teaching research skills as described in Sections 7–9. To introduce each new genre, you may wish to use the overarching lesson (page 4) as your instructional frame.

Personal Responses to Literature

Personal responses to literature can make an excellent introduction to opinion writing. Attending to the key structural elements of an opinion piece, students may use any of the following formats to respond to a story, poem, or informational text.

Grades K–1

- Students draw a picture to help show what the text was about and then express an opinion about it orally (small group or whole class).

- Students draw a picture and write or dictate to show an opinion about a text. The writing is compiled into a class book.

Grades 2–5

- Students create a blurb for a professionally published or student-created book.

- Students create bulleted notes or a poster for a book talk to be delivered to the class.

- Students create a page for a class literary magazine, expressing a personal opinion about a book.

- Students create a blog that states an opinion about a book and ask classmates to respond with agreement or disagreement.

Book Reviews

A book review, created with a somewhat more formal tone than a personal response to literature, is an evaluative piece that may come in the form of a poster, video clip, or written narrative. To guide students to write a book review, show them how to do the following:

- Tell something about the content without giving away the ending.

- Tell what was great or not so great about the piece.

Opportunity to Emphasize Language Standard 3

> Use a formal discourse/register for book talks, video clips, and written reviews. This is different from informally talking with one friend about a book.

> Choose effective, precise words and phrases.

- Tell what the author and illustrator did well or not well.

- Tell who should read this piece and why.

As with any type of opinion piece, the author provides details and reasons that help to explain the opinion.

Literary Essays

Literary essays might sound like something beyond the skill level of most elementary students, but this genre can in fact be in tune with their developing capabilities. We generally don't introduce literary essays until around third or fourth grade because to work within the genre requires a merging of skills in the area of both opinion writing and text analysis—which take some time and instruction to develop.

A literary essay generally calls on students to make a claim or statement about a text that goes beyond the evaluative type statement seen in a book review. So, instead of considering *What did you like?*, students consider questions such as *What is the theme? What lesson do you think the author intended to teach? What kind of person is this character? How did this character change over time?* While literary essays aren't designed to "persuade" per se, students must provide reasons for the point they are developing.

To get started, students might be asked to identify a theme in a book such as Dr. Seuss' *Sneetches* or *The Lorax,* or Jerry Spinelli's *Wringer* or *Maniac McGee*, and show how it is developed through a character's experiences. Or they might identify how a character changes over time and then describe how the author develops that progression. Writing a literary essay is much more than writing for the sake of demonstrating knowledge or understanding. Such an experience pushes students into considering literature through fresh new lenses and creates rich material for discussion, thus enhancing the potential for appreciation and enjoyment.

Persuasive Letters

From the time they are very young, children want to have a say about many aspects of their lives, and persuasive letters are a viable means for such expression. Students just moving into opinion writing will best feel the impact if they write for a personal audience, such as a letter to the teacher telling how they feel about a particular part of classroom life or a card for a family member expressing reasons they appreciate that person. As students develop their skill, they can also develop pieces that reflect new content they are learning in the classroom and write for a more broad audience such as the readership of a grade-level, school, or local newspaper; a letter to a community member; or a letter to an administrator in the school.

Opportunity to Emphasize
Language Standard 3

❯ Use a formal discourse/ register that will persuade effectively without offending.

❯ Choose precise words and phrases to make key points and keep audience attention.

❯ Use "showing" words rather than "telling" words.

❯ Choose words that will help the reader keep an open mind even if there is a tendency toward disagreement.

Persuasive Essays

Children write persuasive essays to make a case for something they care about. Rather than being directed at a particular person or a particular audience (such as a teacher or the readers of a local newspaper), persuasive essays are written for anyone who may be interested in picking up the piece. Persuasive essays can be published as:

- a page for a class book focused on general issues deemed important by the students

- a page for a class book focused on a particular topic from the content-area curriculum (These books are fun to pass among grade-level classrooms because students across grade levels are typically studying the same content.)

- a blog that states an opinion and asks the audience (often classmates or grademates) to respond with agreement or disagreement

Blogs

A blog is a public forum that students can use to express viewpoints and opinions. If your school doesn't have a system in place, but you have access to computers, try Edublogs (http://edublogs.org). This website offers a free system that is set up for educational purposes and includes easy-to-follow guidelines for implementing the entire blogging process. Your blogs can be set for complete privacy (such as allowing only the teacher to log in, or only the teacher and students, or only the teacher and other teachers in the school). Before getting started, check with your administrative office to learn about any existing tools or policies your school may have to guide the process.

In relation to Writing Anchor 1, students working in small groups can use a blogging system to do the following:

- Write an opinion statement. Post the statement, asking for written comments from other groups or from another class.

- Create a survey asking for classmates' opinions on a topic, an issue, or a text (two to four questions). Use the results from one of the questions to create an opinion statement (with reasons) that represents viewpoints from the class.

- Post an opinion on a topic or text. Other groups develop and post responses, giving reasons for their opinions. Each group then leads an oral discussion on the issue.

Opportunity to Emphasize
Language Standard 3

> Use a formal discourse/register that will gently persuade without offending. It helps to try to show awareness of multiple perspectives and avoid implying that others have "bad" ideas or practices.

> Choose effective, precise words and phrases.

Opportunity to Emphasize
Language Standard 3

> Use an informal but smart-sounding register that will persuade effectively without offending.

> Choose engaging, precise words and phrases to make key points and keep audience attention.

> Choose words that will help the reader keep an open mind even if there may be a tendency toward disagreement.

Persuasive Video or Photo Documentaries

Photo and video documentaries are an engaging medium for expressing opinions about issues and events. If you have access to digital technology (camera or video) students can create multimedia opinion pieces. Consider the following:

- Work with students to generate opinion statements about life in the classroom, school, or schoolyard. For example, "Wet shoes should not be worn into the classroom," "We don't have many great books in our classroom," or "Littering on or near the playground is a bad idea." The task for this project is to use photographs with captions to *show the reasons* behind the opinions. Give student teams a camera and allow each team to take three to five photos. The group composes a written opinion piece with an introduction that states the opinion, reasons (supported by photos and connected with linking words), and a conclusion.

- Show students how to use video technology to record themselves making a case for something they feel is important. The group writes an engaging introduction with an opinion statement to read aloud on camera; each group member responds on camera with a concise reason for the opinion; and the group writes a closing statement to read aloud on camera.

Advertisements

Persuasion is all around us, especially in advertising. After examining advertising materials with your guidance (see Figure 1–19 for a starter set of questions to explore), students can write their own ads. Interesting advertising genres to explore with elementary students include websites or brochures advertising places to visit; advertisements for foods; and advertisements for toys, video games, and electronics. Desktop publishing programs can be used to publish the final pieces, or students can create their own designs on paper. If using desktop publishing, you may wish to set up the template for the students.

Figure 1–19

Questions for Evaluating Advertisements

- What is the advertiser trying to sell?

- Describe what stands out most for you on this advertisement.

- Do you think this advertisement is aimed at children, adults, or both? How can you tell?

- What are the people pictured doing? Why do you suppose the advertisers chose this? What does the illustrator do to convince?

- Find a place where the product/place is described. What language is used to convince?

- Do you think the advertisers have done a good job of selling the product? Why or why not?

TEXT TYPES AND PURPOSES

English Language Arts Standards: **Writing Anchor 2**

Writing Anchor 2: Write informative/explanatory texts to examine and convey complex ideas and information clearly and accurately through the effective selection, organization, and analysis of content.

Kindergarten	First	Second	Third	Fourth	Fifth
Use a combination of drawing, dictating, and writing to compose informative/ explanatory texts in which they name what they are writing about and supply some information about the topic.	Write informative/ explanatory texts in which they name a topic, supply some facts about the topic, and provide some sense of closure.	Write informative/ explanatory texts in which they introduce a topic, use facts and definitions to develop points, and provide a concluding statement or section.	Write informative/ explanatory texts to examine a topic and convey ideas and information clearly. **a.** Introduce a topic and group related information together; include illustrations when useful to aiding comprehension. **b.** Develop the topic with facts, definitions, and details. **c.** Use linking words and phrases (e.g., *also, another, and, more, but*) to connect ideas within categories of information. **d.** Provide a concluding statement or section.	Write informative/ explanatory texts to examine a topic and convey ideas and information clearly. **a.** Introduce a topic clearly and group related information in paragraphs and sections; include formatting (e.g., headings), illustrations, and multimedia when useful to aiding comprehension. **b.** Develop the topic with facts, definitions, concrete details, quotations, or other information and examples related to the topic. **c.** Link ideas within categories of information using words and phrases (e.g., *another, for example, also, because*). **d.** Use precise language and domain-specific vocabulary to inform about or explain the topic. **e.** Provide a concluding statement or section related to the information or explanation presented.	Write informative/ explanatory texts to examine a topic and convey ideas and information clearly. **a.** Introduce a topic clearly, provide a general observation and focus, and group related information logically; include formatting (e.g., headings), illustrations, and multimedia when useful to aiding comprehension. **b.** Develop the topic with facts, definitions, concrete details, quotations, or other information and examples related to the topic. **c.** Link ideas within and across categories of information. **d.** Use precise language and domain-specific vocabulary to inform about or explain the topic. **e.** Provide a concluding statement or section related to the information or explanation presented.

Decision Tree for **Writing** ANCHOR 2

Is now a good time for focused instruction in relation to Writing Anchor 2?

Anchor 2 requires that students *write informative/explanatory texts*. When your students have information they would benefit from exploring and sharing through writing, it is recommended that you implement three types of instruction:

Demonstration	Collaborative Engagement	Independent Application
Page 38	Page 64	Page 67

An initial overarching demonstration occurs first, followed by a formative assessment. After analyzing the assessment data, you can use the information below to decide what to teach next and whether this instruction is needed for the whole class or small groups.

Minilessons

After the overarching lesson and formative assessment, choose from the following based on student needs:

- Finding a Meaningful Topic (page 54)
- Organizing and Managing a Piece (page 54)
- Developing the Content (page 56)
- Using Illustrations and Other Media (page 58)
- Crafting a Title (page 59)
- Crafting a Strong Introduction (page 59)
- Providing a Sense of Closure (page 60)

Collaborative Engagement

Use the following experiences to encourage deeper consideration of key writing concepts:

- Analyzing and Evaluating Writing Samples from the Classroom (page 64)
- Analyzing and Evaluating Mentor Text (page 65)
- Conferring with the Teacher (page 65)
- Conferring with Peers (page 65)

Independent Application

When you have students ready to explore new genres of informative/explanatory writing, consider the following:

- All-About Books (page 67)
- How-to Pieces (page 67)
- Informational Articles (page 67)
- Research and Lab Reports (page 67)
- Informational Web Pages (page 68)
- Oral Presentations (page 68)
- Informational Documentaries (page 70)
- Newsletters and Memos (page 71)

You may cycle back through these applications throughout the year, addressing techniques for revising and editing as described in Sections 4 and 5; bringing in technology as described in Section 6, and teaching research skills as described in Sections 7–9.

Demonstration

Anchor 2 requires that students write *informative/explanatory* or "informational" texts. Informational texts can be composed in varied formats, such as books, news articles, research reports, lab reports, instructions, web pages, and memos. This text type serves numerous functions in the workplace and the community and it can be quite relevant in the elementary setting as well. Even the youngest students have information worth sharing and can benefit from learning to do so through informational genres. Along with being a valuable means of communication for children, informational writing is a well-recognized way to develop and firm up their content-area understandings.

When you are ready to begin the instructional process, it is recommended that you provide an overarching demonstration lesson that gives students a general idea of what to include in an informational piece. Then, see what they do with the text type at hand. We need to get students writing—and to observe their writing—in order to know how to best shape and detail our further instruction.

The overarching lesson below features a set of tools for teaching a flexible beginning structure for an informational piece, along with an assessment tool to help you identify key next steps for instruction. The lesson may be implemented as many times as needed, and may be used any time a new genre or format for informational writing is introduced.

Overarching Lesson

To prepare for the lesson, have in mind a specific format (such as a news article or a page for an *all-about* book) and a topic related to your curriculum. You will be demonstrating how to structure an informational piece appropriate to your grade level and then providing time and support for students to write their own.

1. **Purpose**

    - Tell students that you will be showing them how to write an informational text, and that the purpose for informational writing is to share information or teach about a concept.

    - Tell students the *format* and *topic* you will be using for your demonstration and let them know that they will be writing a piece in the same format and choosing a similar topic.

2. **Expectations.** Briefly show students the expectations for informational writing at your grade level. Use an enlarged checklist

(Figure 2–1) or a map that includes the required grade-level components (Figures 2–2 to 2–6). Just quickly point out what is generally included in such a piece so that students have a sense of the text type before they write. Too much emphasis on structure can lead students to plugging in words just to be "done" rather than allowing them to experiment with ideas in a way that has meaning for them.

3. **Demonstration**

- Use either the checklist or the map as a guide to show students how you play around with the organization and lay out your ideas. Either *tell* students what you plan to include, showing where on the page you would place your ideas, or *draft the text as they observe*. Keep your demonstration in line with your students' developing capabilities. For example, in kindergarten you might create a page for a class book, showing how to include detail in the drawing and how to label key elements of the drawing and write a short description using invented spelling and learned words. In grades 3 to 5, you may be showing how to include a page for a website that includes extended narrative and other features shown on the checklist. *Note*: Students need not include every item on the checklist (facts, definitions, details, quotations, and examples) in every piece.

- Tell students that the parts you are showing them should be used in their own writing because they will help to build a complete piece. *Note for using the maps:* Students may use a map as their *only draft* or as their *plan*, composing the more formal piece after all of the ideas have been laid out. Before asking students to create a piece from material laid out on a map, demonstrate the process, emphasizing concepts such as paragraphing and linking words.

4. **Student Writing**

- Assign students to write a piece within the same format and general topic area you have demonstrated. Before sending them off, get them started brainstorming specific topic possibilities or have them work in teams to brainstorm.

- Arrange adequate time for students to write. Let students know that this is a "show what you know" piece that you will use to inform your next steps in instruction.

For English Learners

Work with English learners in light of their specific topics to ensure they have an idea of how to proceed. For example, you might:

- Ask the student to talk about what the piece will address, and then collaboratively construct the language for the introduction or topic statement, providing support with vocabulary and syntax. Then ask the student to articulate what will go into the rest of the piece, and jot down vocabulary and syntax as appropriate before sending the student off to write.

- Get the student started with ideas for language to use to start each section. (*Polar bears live. . . . Polar bears eat. . . . Polar bear mothers. . . .*)

- Have the student describe what is to be written. Jot down any key syntax or vocabulary that could use support.

5. **Assessment.** Collect each student's writing and evaluate the set to determine how well your students are meeting the Anchor 2 expectations for your grade level. Using a class record (Figures 2–7 to 2–12) will offer an overview of what the class needs and will show individual students' growth from a pre- to a postassessment.

Using Assessment to Inform Instruction

To continue your instruction after the initial assessment, first decide whether students will move on to a new piece or revise/continue to work with the current piece. As you provide minilessons, students need to have specific pieces in mind to which they can apply the concepts you are teaching. If the class record shows that most students could use instruction in a particular area, it is advisable to keep the class together for the minilessons. If the class record shows varied needs, then provide a mix of minilessons, pulling students in to work with you depending on the needs they have demonstrated. The decision tree on page 37 can help you to set your course.

Figure 2–1

CHECKLIST OF EXPECTATIONS FOR WRITING ANCHOR 2

Kindergarten

❏ Names the topic.

❏ Supplies some information about the topic.

Grade 1

❏ Names the topic.

❏ Supplies some facts about the topic.

❏ Provides closure.

Grade 2

❏ Introduces the topic.

❏ Uses facts and definitions to develop points.

❏ Provides a conclusion.

Grade 3

❏ Introduces the topic. Groups related information together. Includes illustrations as useful.

❏ Develops the topic with facts, definitions, and details.

❏ Uses linking words and phrases.

❏ Provides a conclusion.

Grade 4

❏ Introduces the topic. Groups related information by paragraphs and sections. Includes formatting, illustrations, and multimedia as useful.

❏ Develops the topic with facts, definitions, details, quotations, or other information and examples.

❏ Links ideas within categories of information.

❏ Uses precise language and domain-specific vocabulary.

❏ Provides a conclusion.

Grade 5

❏ Introduces the topic. Provides a general observation and focus, grouping related information logically. Includes formatting, illustrations, and multimedia as useful.

❏ Develops the topic with facts, definitions, details, quotations, or other information and examples.

❏ Links ideas within and across categories of information.

❏ Uses precise language and domain-specific vocabulary.

❏ Provides a conclusion.

Figure 2–2

Information Map: Kindergarten

Name: _____ Date: _____

Topic

Information

Figure 2–3

Information Map: Kindergarten

Name: _____ Date: _____

Topic: _____

Pictures

_____

_____

_____

_____

_____

_____

Figure 2–4

Information Map: Grades 1–2

ANCHOR

2

Name: _____ Date: _____

Picture

Introduction

Information

Closing

Figure 2–5

Information Map: Grades 1–2

Name: _____ Date: _____

(Introduction) _____

_____

_____

_____

_____

_____

_____

_____

_____

_____

(Closing)

_____

_____

Figure 2–6

Information Map: Grades 3–5

Name: _____ Date: _____

Introduction to Topic

Category of Information

Category of Information

Facts, Definitions, Details, Examples, Quotations
(You may use sticky notes here.)

Facts, Definitions, Details, Examples, Quotations
(You may use sticky notes here.)

ANCHOR

2

Figure 2–6 (*continued*)

Information Map: Grades 3–5

Category of Information

Facts, Definitions, Details, Examples, Quotations
(You may use sticky notes here.)

Category of Information

Facts, Definitions, Details, Examples, Quotations
(You may use sticky notes here.)

Conclusion

Figure 2–7

Class Record for Informative/Explanatory Writing: Kindergarten

Student Names	Grade-Level Expectations			
	Names the topic.		Supplies some information about the topic.	
	Date	Date	Date	Date

0 = Not Present   **1 = Could Use Development**   **2 = Developed**

ANCHOR 2

Figure 2–8

Class Record for Informative/Explanatory Writing: Grade 1

Student Names	Grade-Level Expectations					
	Names the topic.		Supplies some facts about the topic.		Provides closure.	
	Date	Date	Date	Date	Date	Date

0 = Not Present   1 = Could Use Development   2 = Developed

Figure 2–9

Class Record for Informative/Explanatory Writing: Grade 2

Student Names	Grade-Level Expectations					
	Introduces the topic.		Uses facts and definitions to develop points.		Provides a conclusion.	
	Date	Date	Date	Date	Date	Date

0 = Not Present   **1 = Could Use Development**   **2 = Developed**

Figure 2–10

Class Record for Informative/Explanatory Writing: Grade 3

Student Names	Grade-Level Expectations							
	Introduces the topic. Groups related information together. Includes illustrations as useful.		Develops the topic with facts, definitions, and details.		Uses linking words and phrases.		Provides a conclusion.	
	Date	Date	Date	Date	Date	Date	Date	Date

ANCHOR 2

0 = Not Present   **1 = Could Use Development**   **2 = Developed**

Figure 2–11

Class Record for Informative/Explanatory Writing: Grade 4

Student Names	Grade-Level Expectations									
	Introduces the topic. Groups related information by paragraphs and sections. Includes formatting, illustrations, and multimedia as useful.		Develops the topic with facts, definitions, details, quotations, or other information and examples.		Links ideas within categories of information.		Uses precise language and domain-specific vocabulary.		Provides a conclusion.	
	Date	Date	Date	Date	Date	Date	Date	Date	Date	Date

0 = Not Present   1 = Could Use Development   2 = Developed

Figure 2–12

Class Record for Informative/Explanatory Writing: Grade 5

Student Names	Grade-Level Expectations									
	Introduces the topic. Provides a general observation and focus, grouping related information logically. Includes formatting, illustrations, and multimedia as useful.		Develops the topic with facts, definitions, details, quotations, or other information and examples.		Links ideas within categories of information.		Uses precise language and domain-specific vocabulary.		Provides a conclusion.	
	Date	Date	Date	Date	Date	Date	Date	Date	Date	Date

ANCHOR 2

0 = Not Present   **1 = Could Use Development**   **2 = Developed**

Minilessons

Your initial observations and assessments will uncover some specific areas in which you want to provide additional instruction—either for certain students or the whole class. The minilessons may be implemented with small groups or the whole class.

Finding a Meaningful Topic

Topics for informational writing should be carefully chosen. Students should write on topics that will lead to their building a meaningful and coherent body of knowledge and understanding in relation to the developing curriculum. Topics may also come from children's interests outside of school. Allowing choice within each project will yield the most engaged writing and will leave students with the opportunity to teach other children about something they aren't already exploring on their own. To prepare for the lesson, decide on a general topic area for the class. This could be specific, as in *animals* or *fractions* or less specific, as in *things I could teach* or *things I know a lot about*.

1. Secure a writer's notebook that you can use for demonstration. Show students how to reserve a page for recording topic ideas for informational writing. As they observe, start a list of possible topics for your own writing that fall within the general area you want them to explore. For example, if students engaged in a study of *sharing the planet* have been assigned to *research an animal of choice*, generate a list of possible animals for your own writing. Use the lesson to show ways of brainstorming topic ideas and then narrowing based on relevance and interest.

2. Provide a writer's notebook for each student. Give students time to work with a partner or team to record at least three of their own ideas. (Kindergarten students may sketch their ideas.) Depending on your focus, you might have students browse through some recently read texts related to the topic area. *Note:* As an alternative to creating individual topic lists, develop a working list of possibilities with the whole class. Students could then choose topics from the list or generate their own similar possibilities.

Organizing and Managing a Piece

Children's informational writing often ends up with a lot of good ideas in a mixed-up order, or with a lot of ideas, only some of which relate directly to the topic at hand. This can stem in part from writing without planning. To support students in learning to plan for a coherent piece, demonstrate working with any of the organizational strategies that follow, and then provide opportunities for students to try the process themselves. IMPORTANT: As they move from planning to drafting, be sure to emphasize the incorporation of linking words (such as *another*, *also*, *for example*, and *in contrast*) to ensure a coherent piece.

USING ASSIGNED CATEGORIES OR HEADINGS. Depending on the assignment, it often works well to assign categories or headings. For example, if all of the students are writing about an animal of their choosing, they might be assigned to use some or all of the following headings: Physical Characteristics, Habitat, Distribution, Diet, Predators, Survival, Life Cycle. Having a set of categories to organize a piece makes the writing manageable, and this type of guidance provides a stepping-stone for students learning to create their own categories. As they begin to write within categories, show them how to use linking words and phrases (such as *also*, *another*, *more*, and *in contrast*) to create coherence and flow.

DEVELOPING CATEGORIES. With guidance, students can learn to create their own categories to organize their writing. As they begin planning, ask them to list, tell, or sketch what they think is interesting about the topic or what parts of the topic they want to teach about. For example, a student planning a piece about dance listed the following:

> How to stretch
>
> How to do a leap
>
> How to do a turn
>
> How to do a cartwheel

After creating their lists, students consider which of their items would make sense as subheads and begin to collect information and write accordingly.

USING A PLANNING MAP. A planning map can be a useful tool for gathering and organizing ideas before writing. Show students how you use Figure 2–2, 2–3, 2–4, 2–5, or 2–6 to plan a piece of your own writing. You can use the map to jot down your ideas or to tell students what you are considering writing about. As students begin to take their ideas from map to narrative, show them how to incorporate linking words and phrases (such as *another*, *because*, and *especially*) to ensure flow and coherence. Reading the narrative aloud can help students to get a feel for where linking words are needed.

SHARPENING THE FOCUS. There will be times when students will start with a broad, unmanageable topic such as *sports* or *the presidency* that needs to be narrowed. You can support students in narrowing their topics by showing them how to sharpen the focus.

1. First, set the parameters as you always do. "We're all working on (writing an all-about book/designing a web page/contributing a page for a class informational book) focused on _____. You get to choose your own topic but I've noticed that some of the topics need sharpening."

2. Tell the students that a piece becomes most manageable when the writer has a sharp focus in mind whether writing a book, section, page, or paragraph, and that you will show them a way to go from a broad to a sharp focus when thinking about what to write.

3. Draw an enlarged V shape to use for illustration. Having a visual will help you to refer back to the shape later as students are sharpening their own topics. At the top of the shape, write a general topic, such as basketball. Point out that it would be too much to include everything you know or have read about basketball, and that it will help you to start writing with a sharper focus in mind. Start a second row to jot possible topics such as *how to play*, *most important skills*, *equipment*, or *famous players*. Then show students how you narrow the topic even further with a third row. For example, if you are writing about *how to play*, will you focus on providing a set of rules or will it be a description of how the game progresses? If you are focusing on famous players, will they be contemporary or historic? How many would be doable to write about? Keep narrowing and orally thinking through the focus until the topic feels manageable.

4. Provide time for students to talk with a partner or team using the V shape for brainstorming before moving into their writing.

Developing the Content

Strong informational writing is embedded with content that informs, engages, and creates a rich picture in the reader's mind. To support students in learning to embed a piece with rich content, it helps if they first have a manageable focus (see minilessons on managing the piece and sharpening the focus). When the focus is clear we can guide them to develop the content. Following are some minilesson ideas.

ELABORATION. Demonstrate how to elaborate on a topic by showing students a piece of your work or student work that is unfinished or leaves room for development. For example, show a drawing with little detail or a piece of writing that could really use some examples or explanation. Give students a quick overview of possible ways to elaborate (see sidebar) and then demonstrate just one or two techniques as relevant to developing your current piece. Send students off with plans to elaborate on their topics using the techniques you have demonstrated.

> **Elaboration**
> - facts
> - definitions
> - details
> - examples
> - quotations
> - other information

STRETCHING A STATEMENT. Show students a piece of your writing or student writing that needs development in terms of content or vocabulary. Demonstrate how to expand on a particular statement so that it offers more information. Consider the following lab report from a kindergarten student, which the student expanded with support from the teacher (spellings corrected):

- They hatched.

- We have worms and they hatched.

- We have worms in our classroom and they hatched yesterday morning.

- We have worms in our classroom and they hatched yesterday morning. They are big. One inch.

Send students off with plans to stretch one statement at a time from a piece they are currently working to develop. They may meet with a partner to identify the particular statements needing development or you can help them to identify the statements. As an option, have them underline domain-specific vocabulary (words that are important to the topic) and determine whether a definition is needed.

FREEWRITING OR FREEDRAWING. Freewrites and freedraws can inspire new ideas. Give students a blank piece of paper and exactly three minutes to write or draw everything they can in relation to their topic. (Demonstrate the process first.) They should write or draw anything that comes to mind as long as it relates to their topic. When the three-minute session is over, students work with a peer to talk over and identify at least one idea to develop the piece. To encourage the use of domain-specific vocabulary, ask students to label key elements of their drawings or circle key elements of their writings and then consider whether words that are important to explaining the concept have been included. Students can brainstorm key words that help to explain the content. If the class is working on similar content, use the opportunity to create a word bank representing key vocabulary that might be useful.

READING. Students can often benefit from taking time to read in relation to the topic at hand. During workshop time, many students want to write and may not take adequate time to read and cite information from texts if they are not encouraged or given time to do so. Show students how you read for ideas and highlight or take notes. (For more detail, see Sections 8 and 9). You can give them highlighting tape or sticky notes to mark domain-specific vocabulary that they might use in their own pieces. You may wish to pull students aside to a special area of the classroom designated for reading. This will show them that reading is an important part of the writing process.

Using Illustrations and Other Media

Authors of informational text use illustrations and other media to help explain and clarify concepts. To support your students in expanding their repertoire of skills in this area, it is recommended that you demonstrate one technique at a time, over time, as it fits within your own writing. The particular techniques you demonstrate should be of use within the current focus area for student writing. Common techniques include:

- Pictures with labels or captions
- Clip art with labels or captions
- Photos with labels or captions
- Sideboxes for defining domain-specific vocabulary
- Hyperlinks to a website addresses
- Hyperlink to video captured by students
- Hyperlink to photo captured by students
- Chart with labels and interpretive narrative
- Map with labels and interpretive narrative
- Diagram with labels and interpretive narrative
- Graph with labels and interpretive narrative

As you demonstrate, help students understand that authors and illustrators have a job of teaching their audience, and they use all the media techniques they can to achieve that goal.

Crafting a Title

A strong title for an informational text discloses key information about the content and genre, quite often in a way that makes the piece stand out from any other. (See the titles from Figure 2–13.) Following are some minilessons designed to support children's creation of strong informational text titles.

RATIONALIZING TITLE PREFERENCES. Give partnered students a few minutes to look around the classroom and choose a favorite title from an informational text they have read. Ask that they describe *why they like the title* and *how it enhances the piece*. Use the students' choices to create a list of good titles. Post the list where they can access it for inspiration during writing time. As an alternative to collecting favorite titles, ask partnered students to find an informational text title in the classroom that does not work as well as it could. Have them discuss their rationale for wanting to strengthen it, and suggest a new title.

PRACTICE WITH TITLES. Read aloud a text or subheaded section of a text without showing or telling the title. Have students generate a list of title ideas and vote on the best. Discuss why the student-suggested titles make sense and how they compare with the actual text title.

CONSIDERING TITLES ACROSS GENRES. Give groups of students a collection of titles representing informational texts, poetry, and fiction. Disclose the three categories and ask students to sort the titles and tell why they think each belongs within a certain category. As an alternative, give groups a collection of informational text titles representing different genres, such as newspaper articles, how-to books, and all-about books. Disclose the categories and ask students to sort the titles and tell why they think each belongs within a certain category.

Crafting a Strong Introduction

Teaching students to introduce their readers to the informational pieces they are writing is easy enough: "This book is about the *Edmund Fitzgerald*." "This section shows the parts of a kite." "Noses are important." While such starters serve the important function of introducing the content, each could be improved. The challenge of introducing an informational text is not so much in telling what's there as it is in engaging or grabbing the attention of the reader. A strong introduction to an informational text does both: it introduces the topic *and* hooks the reader.

LEARN FROM PROFESSIONAL AUTHORS. Show students the openings to a small set of informational texts and ask what makes them strong or not strong. (Figure 2–13 provides a recommended set of texts with their opening lines.)

TRY DIFFERENT OPENING TECHNIQUES. Compile a list of three or four techniques for opening an informational text. (You can add to the list over time.) Start with a direct or formulaic introduction so that students can compare it with other techniques. Post the list with a set of examples related to a piece you are currently using for demonstration, discussing the techniques you have listed. (See Figure 2–14.) For whatever piece they are working on, assign students to try out two or three different introductory statements and then work with a peer or team to help determine a favorite.

Providing a Sense of Closure

As early as first grade, students are expected to provide a sense of closure with their written pieces. To help your students learn to provide a rich sense of closure, the following strategies may be implemented.

LEARN FROM PROFESSIONAL AUTHORS. Show the students the endings to a small set of professionally published informational pieces/sections and ask what makes them strong or not strong. Point out that authors typically leave us with something to think about rather than simply summarizing the content of the piece.

TRY DIFFERENT CLOSURE TECHNIQUES. Review a set of closure techniques, using your own writing as an example. Assign students to try two or three different techniques in their own pieces and then work with a partner or team to select a favorite. Figure 2–15 provides some example techniques.

Figure 2–13

Mentor Texts for Informational Writing

Grades K–2	
Jobs (Susan Canizares and Betsy Chessen)	What do people do on the job?
The Snail's Spell (Joanne Ryder)	Imagine you are soft and have no bones inside you.
To Be a Kid (Maya Ajmera and John Ivanko)	To be a kid means . . .
All About Owls (Jim Arnosky)	Have you ever wondered about owls?
What Is a Reptile? (Feana Tu'akoi)	What is a reptile? Let's see . . .
What Lincoln Said (Sarah Thomson)	"The world seemed wider and fairer before me." That was how Abraham Lincoln remembered the day he earned his first dollar.
Grades 3–5	
Just a Second: A Different Way to Look at Time (Steve Jenkins)	A second goes by pretty quickly. In fact, several have passed since you started reading this sentence.
Bones (Steve Jenkins)	Bones are alive.
Maritcha: A Ninteenth-Century American Girl (Tonya Bolden)	Aim high! Stand tall! Be strong! and do! These ideals were sown in the soul of young Maritcha Remond Lyons, a child of New York City's striving class of blacks in the mid-1800s.
Poop: A Natural History of the Unmentionable (Nicola Davies)	Grownups are shy about it . . . Horses ignore it . . . Dogs like to sniff it . . . And babies do it in their diapers. . . .
When Fish Got Feet, Sharks Got Teeth, and Bugs Began to Swarm: A Cartoon Prehistory of Life Long Before Dinosaurs (Hannah Bonner)	What, you don't recognize Pennsylvania? That's not surprising. Nowadays the countryside in Pennsylvania is covered in greenery, but 430 million years ago the tallest plants around the world would have been knee-high to a grasshopper, had there been any grasshoppers.
After the Last Dog Died: The True-Life, Hair-raising Adventure of Douglas Mawson and His 1911–1914 Antarctic Expedition (Carmen Bredesen)	**December 2, 1911** Douglas Mawson leaned on the rail of the ship Aurora, looking down at the crowd gathered below. . . . Mawson and his crew of 30 men were headed for an unexplored region of Antarctica, the coldest, windiest continent on Earth. They would not be back for more than a year if they came back at all.

Figure 2–14

Techniques for Informational Leads

- **Direct statement**: This book is about tap dancing. You will learn about tap shoes, tap floors, and tap steps.

- **"Draw-in" question**: Have you ever had tap shoes on your feet? Would you like to try? First, there are some things you should know. Read on and you will learn about tap shoes, tap floors, and tap steps.

- **Fact-based question**: What kind of shoe has metal on the sole? What kind of shoe loves a wooden floor? You guessed it! Taps! This book is about tap dancing. You will learn about tap shoes, tap floors, and tap steps.

- **Fact or detail**: Tap shoes didn't always have metal on the soles but they do now. The metal is called the *tap* and it's the most important part of the shoe. Read on to learn more about tap shoes, tap floors, and tap steps.

- **Comparison**: Ballet shoes are quiet. Tap shoes are not. This book is about tap dancing. You will learn about tap shoes, tap floors, and tap steps.

- **Quotation**: "Take off those tap shoes!" Tap shoes. You love them or you hate them. I love them and I am going to teach you about tap shoes, tap floors, and tap steps.

- **Scene**: The auditorium is quiet except for the click click click of three girls entering the stage. Their tap shoes are covered with red, gold, and silver sequins. A lot of preparation has gone into this day.

- **Connection to the audience**: If you have ever been around a tap dancer, you know how irresistible tap shoes can be. Let's find out why.

- **Observation from the senses**: Tap shoes sound like *ba da lump bump bump, ba da lump bump bump*. If you like rhythm, then read on!

Figure 2–15

Closure Techniques

- **Summary**: Summarize the content, presenting the information through a new angle rather than repeating everything directly.

- **Reaction or feeling**: Tell how you feel about the content.

- **Image description**: Describe a visual or sensory image related to the content.

- **Image**: Include a visual image (photo, drawing, clip art) related to the overall message.

- **Quotation**: Present an interesting quotation or fact related to what you have written. You might need to write something before or after the quotation/fact so that it makes sense to the reader.

- **Encouragement to reflect**: End with a statement that encourages readers to keep thinking about the concept.

- **Encouragement to act**: End with a statement that encourages the taking of some action (such as using less fossil fuel or continuing to look for real-life uses of math).

- **Question**: End with a question that encourages readers to keep thinking about the concept.

Collaborative Engagement

To enhance their understanding of key concepts for writing informational text, arrange for students to engage in collaborative analysis and evaluation experiences, peer conferences, and teacher conferences.

Analyzing and Evaluating Writing Samples from the Classroom

After teaching students about key structural elements to include in their informational writing (as per grade-level standards), give groups a sample of student writing (or use teacher writing if you don't yet have a student sample) and ask them to analyze it in light of particular criteria. When working with Anchor 2, select from questions such as those featured in Figure 2–16. After groups meet, you can bring the whole class back together for a follow-up discussion.

Figure 2–16

Questions for Analyzing and Evaluating Informative/Explanatory Pieces

Grades K–5

- What is the topic of this piece/section/page? Is it easy to locate?
- What does the author teach about the topic? Do we have questions?
- What do the illustrations teach? What details could be added?

Grades 1–5

- How does the author introduce the topic? What techniques does the author use to hook the reader?
- How does the author develop the topic with facts, definitions, details, quotations, or other information and examples? What questions do we have?
- How did the author close the piece?

Grades 3–5

- How is this organized? What headings are used? What other types of formatting are used?
- What is the purpose of the illustrations or other media? Is there anything that could be added or done to improve these?
- What linking words are used to create clarity and flow? Are there places in which the sequence is not clear?

Grades 4–5

- What vocabulary is important within this piece? What is provided to help determine the definitions?

Analyzing and Evaluating Mentor Text

An important force in children's development as writers is having opportunities to read and view text created by professional authors. Using specific questions to analyze the author's craft can open students to new ideas to consider for their own writing.

1. Show students how to reserve a section of the writing notebook to record great ideas or language from mentor texts. They need not record all of the ideas encountered, but should instead focus on their favorites.

2. After the students read, view, or listen to a text, set them up in groups and give each a copy of the text, directing them to a specific section as appropriate. Assign the groups to work through one to three guiding questions, such as those featured in Figure 2–16. You can differentiate by having different groups work with different questions or texts. Encourage students to jot ideas in their notebooks (or require each student to record at least one idea to possibly share at the end of the group meeting).

3. Arrange time for the groups to report their findings and observations.

Conferring with the Teacher

Conferences are important for all student writers. Conference time may be used to listen to students talk and help them articulate their topics and ideas, to teach a specific strategy, or for a quick follow-up to see how newly learned strategies are being incorporated. As a rule of thumb, keep the focus on *teaching the writer* rather than *perfecting the piece*. It can be tempting to help the student create a flawless piece, but it is generally more beneficial to focus on one key concept or strategy that the student can carefully consider and internalize.

When conferring in relation to Anchor 2, keep your focus on Anchor 2 objectives. Organizing the conference with a predictable set of prompts and questions can help students know what to expect and be ready to show you their thinking. See Figure 2–17.

Conferring with Peers

Children can be very capable and responsible responders to their peers' writing, especially when they are given some starting expectations for their conversations. After they have some experience conferring with you, coach them to work in peer conferences through any of the processes featured in Figure 2–18.

Figure 2–17

Conference Routine

- **Open the conversation**. *How are things going with this piece? What are you teaching your audience? Is there something you need help with?*

- **Identify notable strengths.** *This part of your drawing helps me learn about the topic because. . . . Your introduction draws me in because. . . . I feel like I really understand what this is going to be about because. . . . Your topic is well-developed because. . . . This conclusion works so well because. . . . It seems important that you have defined this word because. . . .*

- **Identify one teaching point.** *What do you think you should revise or do next from here? Can you show me how you will start? Or I have one thing I want you to develop and I'm going to help you get started.*

- **Send the student away with something manageable to develop.** *Let's get you started on this and then next time we meet we can talk about how it's going.*

Figure 2–18

Peer Conference Plans

- Ask the author to read the piece with you and tell you about one part that teaches something important. Then tell the author about one part you think teaches something important.

- Tell the author what you feel is the biggest strength and offer one suggestion. Help the author get started on the suggestion.

- Write a response to your peer on a sticky note. Tell one strength and offer one suggestion.

- Ask the author to tell you more details about one part of the picture/ illustration or one part of the writing. Help the author with specific ideas to get started on adding details about that part, if needed.

- Together with the author, look at our informational writing checklist (see Figure 2–1) and find all the key parts. Are all the parts present?

- Together with the author, ask: Does everything make sense? Help the author get started on fixing any parts that do not make sense.

Independent Application

The independent application section offers suggestions for helping students move into different genres of informational writing. You may cycle back through these applications throughout the year, addressing techniques for revising and editing as described in Sections 4 and 5, bringing in technology as described in Section 6, and teaching research skills as described in Sections 7–9. To introduce each new genre, you may wish to use to the overarching lesson (page 38) as your instructional frame.

All-About Books

All-about books are excellent tools for supporting content-area learning. They specify a topic and address it in depth. They may be written across the content areas: science, math, social studies, music, art, health, or physical education. Students may create their own books or they may make one- or two-page contributions for a class book. Or teams may work together on a book, with different students taking responsibility for different sections. All-about books are typically written using subheads, which helps to keep the content manageable.

How-to Pieces

How-to pieces differ from all-about pieces in that the focus is on providing instructions or guidance rather than solely on providing information. How-to pieces generally come in the form of instructions, directions, steps, or procedures. Sometimes a list of materials or ingredients is included. Sometimes the steps of the process are numbered. Sometimes illustrations are included. An important strategy to teach in how-to writing is to consider whether the sequence has been made clear. Students may show sequence through numbering, formatting on the page, or using temporal words and phrases.

Informational Articles

Informational articles can take the form of informative/explanatory pieces typically found in magazines or on websites for kids, or more brief content pieces such as one-paragraph clips of information found on the web. They are generally written in a formal discourse, as the audience is broader than the classroom setting.

Research and Lab Reports

Research and lab reports generally emerge from the science or social studies curriculum. Whether children are testing the capacity of objects to sink

> **Opportunity to Emphasize**
> **Language Standard 3**
> ❯ Use a formal discourse/ register for informational articles.
> ❯ Choose precise words and phrases.

or float, comparing conditions for growing plants, documenting bird sightings, or collecting opinions on an upcoming election, there is an acceptable set of procedures for reporting the findings. Students should include:

- a topic

- a question

- a prediction or hypothesis (if applicable)

- procedures

- observations

- conclusions

Demonstrate the scientific processes as well as the writing processes before setting students off to write. Research reports are often of use to the whole class in terms of supporting content-area learning and are ideal for oral presentations. The requirements for structure provide a helpful frame for students learning to present a set of ideas orally. Sections 7, 8, and 9 contain more detail.

Informational Web Pages

Informational web page writing can be geared toward any content area. Content may include any combination of written narrative, photos, time-lapse photography, captions, clip art, images from digital drawing or painting tools, audio clips, video clips, and the use of text effects (such as varied fonts, shades, and colors). Usually, more than one form of media is included. If you have good online access for creating a website, this is ideal. (Try weebly.com.) If not, a PowerPoint or word-processing program with hyperlinking capability will suffice. Figure 2–19 shows an example of a "website" created using PowerPoint. It includes working links to five documents written by the author of the "site" (all can be kept on classroom computers) as well as a link to an online website. Or if your students have little access to computers, such pieces can be designed completely on paper. Just provide a template and a set of expectations.

Oral Presentations

Oral presentations are an important part of the content-area writing curriculum. Instead of writing a narrative, students write notes (often bulleted points that are shown to the audience) that help them keep their presentation

Figure 2–19

All About Dogs Website Created with PowerPoint

Groups the information into categories

ALL ABOUT DOGS

- Kinds of Dogs.docx
- Playing.docx
- Communicating.docx
- Sleeping.docx
- Eating.docx

Have you ever wanted to learn about dogs? Click on the links to learn about different kinds of dogs and the things dogs like to do.

Introduces topic and provides a focus

Click on this link to learn about training dogs:
http://animal.discovery.com/guides/dogs/dog-training/training/commands.html

EATING

Most dogs should only eat dog food. Table food can be unhealthy for dogs. Table food may not contain all the nutrients a dog needs. Dogs can become malnourished or overweight and this is not healthy. Dogs wish they could eat many things but most dogs should eat dog food.

Develops topic with facts and details; uses precise language and domain-specific vocabulary

Is that some cake on the table?

concise and well-sequenced. Public presentations are doable across the K–5 range. Some examples of topics follow.

Grades K–1

- Show how to draw something.

- Show how to make something.

- Prepare a drawing that helps you describe a concept learned in science, social studies, or math.

Grades 2–5

- Show how to play something.

- Show how to make something.

- Prepare notes for a one-minute talk that illustrates a concept learned in science, social studies, or math. Include visuals to help illustrate the concept.

Informational Documentaries

Photo and video documentaries are an ideal tool for exploring and sharing content knowledge. If you have access to digital technology (camera or video) students can create multimedia informational pieces with images and scenes they have captured.

PHOTO DOCUMENTARIES

Grades K–1

Identify a topic of importance to the curriculum. Ask students (whole class) to guide you in snapping images that will help to teach something about the topic. For example, "How could we show *friendship* or *force* or *motion*?" Print paper copies of the photos. Place students into teams and let each team choose one photo and create labels and captions to describe the concept. Place the finished pieces together in a class book, in a center, or on the classroom wall.

Grades 2–5

Place students into groups. Direct the groups to snap images that will help to teach something about an assigned topic. For example, "How could we show that the motion of an object differs according to the force and mass of the impacting object?"

The group composes a written text with an introduction that lets the audience know what will be learned; a body that teaches about at least one key concept; and a conclusion. They use photographs with captions to illustrate the concepts. Give student teams a camera and allow each team to take three to five photos.

VIDEO DOCUMENTARIES. Show students how to use video technology to record themselves giving a short oral presentation on a key topic within the curriculum. The group writes an introduction to read aloud on camera; each group member offers a fact, definition, detail, quotation, or other piece of information related to the topic; and the group writes a closing statement to read aloud on camera.

Newsletters and Memos

Informational newsletters can be created to let families, other classes, and school staff and administrators know about activities and events in the classroom. Bilingual students can be encouraged to contribute pieces in their first or second language. Possible topics follow:

- What we have been learning in science
- What we have been learning in math
- What we have been learning in social studies
- A new strategy we have learned for reading or writing
- A unique learning experience we've had
- Something we've learned how to do
- Procedures for an upcoming homework assignment
- Information about the field trip we took

**Opportunity to Emphasize
Language Standard 3**

❯ Use a formal discourse/register for the video presentations.

❯ Choose effective, precise words and phrases.

TEXT TYPES AND PURPOSES

ANCHOR 3

English Language Arts Standards: Writing ANCHOR 3

Writing Anchor 3: Write narratives to develop real or imagined experiences or events using effective technique, well-chosen details, and well-structured event sequences.

Kindergarten	First	Second	Third	Fourth	Fifth
Use a combination of drawing, dictating, and writing to narrate a single event or several loosely linked events, tell about the events in the order in which they occurred, and provide a reaction to what happened.	Write narratives in which they recount two or more appropriately sequenced events, include some details regarding what happened, use temporal words to signal event order, and provide some sense of closure.	Write narratives in which they recount a well-elaborated event or short sequence of events, include details to describe actions, thoughts, and feelings, use temporal words to signal event order, and provide a sense of closure.	Write narratives to develop real or imagined experiences or events using effective technique, descriptive details, and clear event sequences. **a.** Establish a situation and introduce a narrator and/or characters; organize an event sequence that unfolds naturally. **b.** Use dialogue and descriptions of actions, thoughts, and feelings to develop experiences and events or show the response of characters to situations. **c.** Use temporal words and phrases to signal event order. **d.** Provide a sense of closure.	Write narratives to develop real or imagined experiences or events using effective technique, descriptive details, and clear event sequences. **a.** Orient the reader by establishing a situation and introducing a narrator and/or characters; organize an event sequence that unfolds naturally. **b.** Use dialogue and description to develop experiences and events or show the responses of characters to situations. **c.** Use a variety of transitional words and phrases to manage the sequence of events. **d.** Use concrete words and phrases and sensory details to convey experiences and events precisely. **e.** Provide a conclusion that follows from the narrated experiences or events.	Write narratives to develop real or imagined experiences or events using effective technique, descriptive details, and clear event sequences. **a.** Orient the reader by establishing a situation and introducing a narrator and/or characters; organize an event sequence that unfolds naturally. **b.** Use narrative techniques, such as dialogue, description, and pacing, to develop experiences and events or show the responses of characters to situations. **c.** Use a variety of transitional words, phrases, and clauses to manage the sequence of events. **d.** Use concrete words and phrases and sensory details to convey experiences and events precisely. **e.** Provide a conclusion that follows from the narrated experiences or events.

Decision Tree for **Writing** ANCHOR 3

Is now a good time for focused instruction in relation to Writing Anchor 3?

Anchor 3 requires that students *write narratives to develop real or imagined experiences or events*. To get your students started with narrative writing, it is recommended that you implement three types of instruction:

Demonstration	Collaborative Engagement	Independent Application
Page 74	Page 101	Page 105

An initial overarching demonstration occurs first, followed by a formative assessment. After analyzing the assessment data, you can use the information below to decide what to teach next and whether this instruction is needed for the whole class or small groups.

Minilessons

After the overarching lesson and formative assessment, choose from the following based on student needs:

- Finding a Topic (page 88)
- Creating an Event Sequence (page 89)
- Establishing the "Situation" (page 90)
- Using Description (page 91)
- Using Dialogue (page 94)
- Using Words and Phrases to Signal Event Order (page 96)
- Pacing (page 97)
- Crafting a Narrative Text Title (page 99)
- Providing a Sense of Closure (page 99)

Collaborative Engagement

Use the following experiences to encourage deeper consideration of key writing concepts:

- Analyzing and Evaluating Writing Samples from the Classroom (page 101)
- Analyzing and Evaluating Mentor Text (page 101)
- Conferring with the Teacher (page 103)
- Conferring with Peers (page 103)

Independent Application

When you have students ready to explore new genres of narrative writing, consider the following.

- Personal Narrative (page 105)
- Memoir (page 105)
- *Testimonio* (page 106)
- Oral History (page 106)
- Biography (page 106)
- Narrative Fiction (page 107)
  - Realistic Fiction
  - Historical Fiction
  - Folktales
  - Fantasy
  - Fables
  - Myths

You may cycle back through these applications throughout the year, addressing techniques for revising and editing as described in Sections 4 and 5; bringing in technology as described in Section 6, and teaching research skills as described in Sections 7–9.

Demonstration

Anchor 3 requires that students *write narratives to develop real or imagined experiences or events*. Narrative texts can be composed in numerous formats, such as personal stories, memoirs, biographies, realistic fiction, folktales, fables, and myths. Early narratives generally feature an illustration accompanied by labels or even a sentence or two, while upper elementary students can be expected to create an extended text featuring the key elements of a good story.

Composing a narrative text is not a far stretch from the type of thinking students have been doing since their earliest days of childhood. From the time they are very young, narratives are woven through children's lives as family members read to them, recount events from their daily lives, talk with them, and tell them stories. Children experience narratives as they watch television, listen to the radio, play computer games, and engage in dramatic play. Even the youngest students are not newcomers to narrative.

In the educational setting, starting each year with a schoolwide exploration of personal narratives offers a way to begin building community within classrooms, and also to consistently track growth for each student over time. Students choose something they have experienced—a single event or situation—and describe it through illustration and/or writing. Because students can draw from what they know to compose these pieces, the writing itself can begin without worrying too much about possible topics. Starting with personal narratives will give you a good feel, right away, for what your students can do with writing.

The overarching lesson features a set of tools for teaching a flexible structure for a narrative, along with an assessment tool to help you identify key next steps for instruction. The lesson may be implemented as many times as needed, and may be used any time a new genre for narrative writing is introduced.

Overarching Lesson

To prepare for this lesson, have in mind a specific genre (such as personal narrative, biography, or folktale). You will be demonstrating, as appropriate to your grade level, how to organize a narrative in your chosen genre and then providing time and support for students to write their own.

1. **Purpose**

   - Tell students that you will be showing them how to write a certain type of story.

   - Tell them the genre you will be demonstrating and let them know that they will be writing a piece in the same genre.

2. **Expectations.** Briefly show students the expectations for narrative writing at your grade level. Use an enlarged checklist (Figure 3–1) or a map that includes the required grade-level components (Figures 3–2, 3–3, and 3–4). Just quickly point out what is generally included in such a piece so that students develop a sense of the text type before they write. *Note:* Students in grades 3 to 5 need not include every item on the form in every piece (dialogue, description, transitional phrases, concrete words, sensory details).

3. **Demonstration**

   - Use either the checklist or the map as a guide to show students how you play around with the organization of and lay out your ideas. This may be as brief as sketching an illustration and articulating the content of one or two sentences you would include or as detailed as outlining your plans for an entire story with characters, setting, problem, and solution. Either *tell* students what you plan to include, showing where on the page you would place your ideas, or *draft the text as they observe.*

   - Tell students that the parts you are showing them should be used in their own writing because they will help to build a complete piece. *Note for using the maps:* Students may use a map as their *only draft* or as their *plan,* composing the more formal piece after all of the ideas have been laid out. Before asking students to create a piece from material laid out on a map, demonstrate the process, emphasizing concepts such as paragraphing and the use of linking words.

For English Learners

Work with English learners in light of their specific topics to ensure they have an idea of how to proceed and what to include. For example, you might:

- Ask the student how the piece should begin, and who is telling the story. Help the student craft the first sentence or two, providing key support with syntax and vocabulary.

- Ask the student what happens in the story and then help to craft the starting language for each key event. Allow the student to fill in the details, providing support as needed.

- Ask the student to draft the entire piece and then review it together for ways to develop or improve the syntax and vocabulary.

You may have other students you want to pull in for step-by-step guidance as well. As a rule of thumb, avoid *always* placing ELs with students who are expressing difficulty with the content. Students learning a new language only sometimes have the same needs as students who are not achieving according to grade-level expectations.

4. **Student Writing**

   - Assign students to write a piece within the genre you have demonstrated. Before sending them off, get them started brainstorming topic possibilities or have them work in teams to discuss possibilities.

   - Arrange adequate time for students to write. Let them know that this is a "show what you know" piece that you will use to inform your next steps in instruction.

5. **Assessment.** Collect each student's writing and evaluate the set to determine how well your class is meeting the Anchor 3 expectations for your grade level. Using a class record (Figures 3–5 to 3–10) will offer an overview of what the class needs and will show individual students' growth from a pre- to a postassessment.

Using Assessment to Inform Instruction

To continue your instruction after the initial assessment, first decide whether students will move on to a new piece or revise the current piece. As you provide minilessons, students need to have specific pieces in mind to which they can apply the concepts you are teaching. If the class record (Figures 3–5 to 3–10) shows that most students could use instruction in a particular area, it is advisable to keep the class together for the minilessons. If the record shows varied needs, then provide a mix of minilessons, pulling students in to work with you depending on the needs they have demonstrated. The decision tree on page 73 can help you to set your course.

Figure 3–1

CHECKLIST OF EXPECTATIONS FOR WRITING ANCHOR 3

Kindergarten

❑ Tells about an event or linked events in the order in which they occurred.

❑ Reacts to what happened.

Grade 1

❑ Recounts two or more appropriately sequenced events.

❑ Includes details about what happened.

❑ Uses words to signal event order.

❑ Provides closure.

Grade 2

❑ Recounts an elaborated event or short sequence of events.

❑ Includes details to describe actions, thoughts, and feelings.

❑ Uses words to signal event order.

❑ Provides closure.

Grade 3

❑ Establishes a situation and narrator and/or characters; organizes an event sequence.

❑ Uses dialogue and descriptions of actions, thoughts, and feelings to develop experiences and events or show responses of characters.

❑ Uses words and phrases to signal event order.

❑ Provides closure.

Grade 4

❑ Establishes a situation and introduces a narrator and/or characters; organizes an event sequence.

❑ Uses dialogue and description to develop events or show responses of characters.

❑ Uses a variety of words and phrases to manage the event sequence.

❑ Uses concrete words and phrases and sensory details.

❑ Provides a conclusion that follows from the narrated events.

Grade 5

❑ Establishes a situation and introduces a narrator and/or characters; organizes an event sequence.

❑ Uses dialogue, description, and pacing to develop events or show responses of characters.

❑ Uses a variety of words, phrases, and clauses to manage the event sequence.

❑ Uses concrete words and phrases and sensory details.

❑ Provides a conclusion that follows from the narrated events.

Figure 3–2

 Event and Reaction Map: Grades K–1

Name: _____ Date: _____

Title: _____

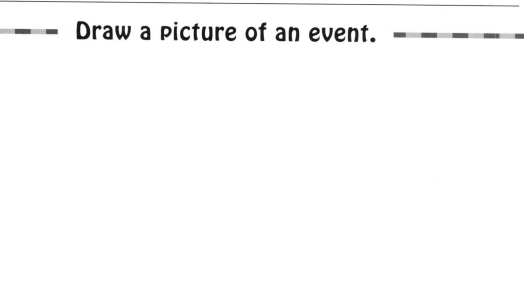

Draw a picture of an event.

Write about the event and tell your reaction.

E _____

_____

_____

_____

R _____

_____

_____

ANCHOR 3

Figure 3–3

Narrative Map: Grades 1–2

Name: _____ Date: _____

Title: _____

First ▶

_____

_____

_____

Next ▶

_____

_____

_____

Next ▶

_____

_____

_____

Closure ⬭ _____

_____

Illustrations

First	Next	Next

Figure 3–4

Narrative Map: Grades 2–5

Name: _____ Date: _____

Title: _____

Establish the situation that will be the focus of the story.

Event

(You may use sticky notes here.)

Event

(You may use sticky notes here.)

Figure 3–4 (*continued*)

Narrative Map: Grades 2–5

Event

(You may use sticky notes here.)

Event

(You may use sticky notes here.)

Conclusion

As you develop the events:

❏ Consider dialogue and description to develop events.

❏ Consider words to show event order.

❏ Consider descriptions from the senses.

Figure 3–5

Class Record for Narrative Writing: Kindergarten

Student Names	Grade-Level Expectations			
	Tells about an event or linked events in the order in which they occurred.		Reacts to what happened.	
	Date	Date	Date	Date

0 = Not Present　　　　**1 = Could Use Development**　　　　**2 = Developed**

ANCHOR 3

Figure 3–6

Class Record for Narrative Writing: Grade 1

Student Names	Grade-Level Expectations							
	Recounts two or more appropriately sequenced events.		Includes details about what happened.		Uses words to signal event order.		Provides closure.	
	Date	Date	Date	Date	Date	Date	Date	Date

0 = Not Present   1 = Could Use Development   2 = Developed

Figure 3–7

Class Record for Narrative Writing: Grade 2

Student Names	Grade-Level Expectations							
	Recounts an elaborated event or short sequence of events.		Includes details to describe actions, thoughts, and feelings.		Uses words to signal event order.		Provides closure.	
	Date	Date	Date	Date	Date	Date	Date	Date

0 = Not Present   **1 = Could Use Development**   **2 = Developed**

Figure 3–8

Class Record for Narrative Writing: Grade 3

Student Names	Grade-Level Expectations							
	Establishes a situation and narrator and/or characters; organizes an event sequence.		Uses dialogue and descriptions of actions, thoughts, and feelings to develop experiences and events or show character views.		Uses words and phrases to signal event order.		Provides closure.	
	Date	Date	Date	Date	Date	Date	Date	Date

ANCHOR 3

0 = Not Present   1 = Could Use Development   2 = Developed

© 2013 by Gretchen Owocki, from *The Common Core Writing Book, K–5*. Portsmouth, NH: Heinemann.

Figure 3–9

Class Record for Narrative Writing: Grade 4

Student Names	Grade-Level Expectations									
	Establishes a situation and introduces a narrator and/or characters; organizes an event sequence.		Uses dialogue and description to develop events or show responses of characters.		Uses a variety of words and phrases to manage the event sequence.		Uses concrete words and phrases and sensory details.		Provides a conclusion that follows from the narrated events.	
	Date	Date	Date	Date	Date	Date	Date	Date	Date	Date

0 = Not Present   1 = Could Use Development   2 = Developed

Figure 3–10

Class Record for Narrative Writing: Grade 5

Student Names	Grade-Level Expectations									
	Establishes a situation and introduces a narrator and/ or characters; organizes an event sequence.		Uses dialogue, description, and pacing to develop events or show responses of characters.		Uses a variety of words, phrases, and clauses to manage the event sequence.		Uses concrete words and phrases and sensory details.		Provides a conclusion that follows from the narrated events.	
	Date	Date	Date	Date	Date	Date	Date	Date	Date	Date

ANCHOR 3

0 = Not Present   **1 = Could Use Development**   **2 = Developed**

Minilessons

Your initial observations and assessments will uncover some specific areas in which you want to provide additional instruction—either for certain students or the whole class. The minilessons may be implemented with small groups or the whole class.

Finding a Topic

Although topics for narrative writing can stem from a broad range of sources, the *characteristics* within the specific narrative genres can help students to narrow their focus. For example, if students are writing biographies, they start with choosing a person. If students are writing a personal narrative, it's a matter of choosing a memorable event. If students are writing a story, it's a matter of envisioning a plot. Assigning a genre will give students a framework for brainstorming the topic or focus.

1. Secure a writer's notebook that you can use for demonstration. Show students how to reserve a page for recording topic ideas or a focus related to the assigned genre. As they observe, start a list of possible topics for your own writing that fall within the genre category you want them to explore. For example, if students are going to be writing biographies about someone they know, make a list of people *you* might write about. If students are going to be writing personal narratives, make a list of situations or events *you* might want to recount. If students are going to be writing fiction pieces, show how you start to brainstorm a plot. Use the lesson to show ways of brainstorming topic ideas and how to begin molding them into something writable.

2. Provide a writer's notebook for each student. Give students time to work with a partner or team to record at least three of their own ideas. Or if they are going to be developing fiction pieces, they might start to brainstorm just one idea with different possible characters and different possible problems/goals for the characters to encounter. *Note:* As an alternative to creating individual topic lists, develop a working list of possibilities with the whole class. Students could choose topics from the list or generate their own similar possibilities.

Creating an Event Sequence

Young writers sometimes set out to compose a narrative from beginning to end. They just start on line one and tell what comes to mind until they reach what feels like an end to the story. But that is seldom the most productive path for creating a piece that the author and readership will find satisfying. To support student development of a rich and coherent narrative, demonstrate one of the planning strategies for creating an event sequence (below), and then provide opportunities for students to try the process themselves. IMPORTANT: As they move from planning to drafting, be sure to emphasize the incorporation of temporal words and phrases (such as *another*, *also*, *for example*, and *in contrast*) to signal event order.

SKETCH THE SEQUENCE. Fold a piece of paper into three sections. Label the sections: *beginning*, *middle*, *end*, and sketch what happens in each part. Use the sketch to help tell the story aloud. Add details to the sketch as needed. Then, use the sketch to guide the writing. Be sure to show how you use key words and phrases to signal the event order.

JOT NOTES ABOUT THE SEQUENCE. Fold a piece of paper into three sections. Label the sections: *beginning*, *middle*, *end*. Jot notes about what happens in each part. Use the notes to practice telling the story aloud, highlighting or circling parts to use and crossing off parts that don't move the piece along. To help with sequencing, it may be useful to number parts of the notes within each section before drafting the story on another paper. Be sure to show how you use key words and phrases to effectively convey the sequence of events.

USE A NARRATIVE MAP. Use a narrative map (Figures 3–2 to 3–4) to think through a story. Point to each section of the map as you talk through what you might include, and then either jot notes on the map or write the story right on the map. As you move from planning to composing, show students how you purposefully use words and phrases to help the audience understand the order of events.

USE STICKY NOTES. List the key events of your narrative on sticky notes. Play around with the order until you have it just right. For example, writing a story about your family dog, you might end up with a set of notes such as the following:

- Sprayed by skunk
- Rinsed with hose

- Scrubbed with dog shampoo

- Scrubbed with tomato juice

- Still smells a little like a skunk

Note: Encouraging a logical order does not mean that students must conform to a chronological time sequence. What we want is for children to learn to present a coherent and interesting message that includes thoughtfully selecting what to tell, staying on track, and keeping the sequence clear.

Establishing the "Situation"

Readers make decisions about text very quickly, which means that the first few lines of a narrative should capture their attention and richly establish the "situation" that will be the focal point of the story. Consider these first lines from some well-known picture books:

> If you could see us sitting here at our old, scratched-up kitchen table, you'd know that we aren't rich.
>
> —Byrd Baylor, *The Table Where Rich People Sit*

> The night Max wore his wolf suit and made mischief of one kind and another his mother called him "WILD THING!" and Max said "I'LL EAT YOU UP!" so he was sent to bed without eating anything.
>
> —Maurice Sendak, *Where the Wild Things Are*

> It was late one winter night, long past my bedtime, when Pa and I went owling.
>
> —Jane Yolen, *Owl Moon*

Each example offers an introduction to the main characters and to the tension or experience they will live through, but does much more than tell it directly. In the present lesson, students gain experience identifying the situation they want to establish, and describing it in a rich way.

1. Compile a list of three or four techniques that student writers can use to establish the situation in narrative text, and post it with a set of examples related to a piece you are currently using for demonstration. (You can add to the list over time.) Start with a direct or formulaic introduction that establishes the situation so that students can compare it with other techniques. See Figure 3–11 for examples. Discuss the techniques.

2. For whatever piece they are working on, assign students to try out two or three different openings and then work with a peer or team to help determine a favorite. They should work toward a lead that establishes the situation and at the same will engage the reader's imagination.

Figure 3–11

Techniques for Establishing the Situation

- **Direct statement**: On Saturday I was hiking with Tomas and Karl and we ran across a skunk.

- **Dialogue**: "Do you smell something?" Karl asked. "Oh, no! Skunnnnk!" Tomas shouted!

- **"Draw-in" question**: Have you ever ridden in a very small car with two yellow labs who have just been sprayed by a skunk?

- **Fact-based question**: Did you know that skunks spray in order to keep off predators? They can spray 10 to 15 feet. And did you also know that skunks can see a dog as a predator?

- **Fact or detail**: Skunks can spray from ten to fifteen feet!

- **Snapshot**: Everything seemed to stop at the same time. Karl stopped walking. Tomas stopped talking. The dogs disappeared into the brush.

- **Connection to the audience**: If you have ever gone driving in the country, you might have smelled a skunk. You know it when you smell it.

- **Series of words**: Dogs. Skunk. Not a good mix.

- **Observation from the senses**: Think sewage. No, worse. Think rotten garbage. No, worse. Try skunk.

Using Description

Description is the heart of narrative writing. The ultimate goal is to create a vivid moving picture in the reader's mind that carries the story along at an appropriate pace. To support your students' development of descriptive writing you can engage with them in the following minilessons.

DETAILING A PERSON, PLACE, OR THING. Using an example from your own writing or student writing, show students how using detail to describe *select* people, places, or things can enhance their writing. The trick is to be *selective*:

- My mom can't believe I play on my trampoline so much. It is old. But it is still bouncy and I love it.

- My mom can't believe I play on my trampoline so much. It sags in the middle. The pad around the rim is torn and peeling. The legs are rusty. But it is still bouncy and I love it.

Not every item in a piece warrants detailing. For example, we would not detail both *mom* and *trampoline* because *trampoline* and not *mom* is the focus of the piece. Good detailing is about selecting just the right parts to develop and move the piece along, and letting all of the other parts maintain their simplicity. When sending students off to develop a piece with detail, it can be very helpful to ensure that they have thoughtfully selected their focus.

ELABORATING AN EVENT. Demonstrate how to select an important event from a piece of writing and elaborate on it one step at a time. Consider the following narrative from a kindergarten student (spellings corrected on the elaboration):

- I wite frnoshr shoping.

- When I went furniture shopping, we bought a table.

- When I went furniture shopping, we bought a table. Now everyone wants to sit in the kitchen.

Help students to identify a sentence or short part of their own work that could use development and send them off to elaborate. Bring the students back together afterward to share their work.

USING SENSORY DETAILS. Use a piece you are currently working on (or a piece of student writing) to demonstrate how to add sensory description. First, list the senses (taste, touch, feel, hear, and see) with your students and then discuss ways you might draw on them to enrich your piece. You can start with just one sentence. For example:

- "I played on the swing set with Tomas."

- "I played on the ice-cold swing set with Tomas. It made our hands sting."

Send students off to work on enhancing their own pieces with sensory detail. You can ask that they start with just one sentence.

SHOWING, NOT TELLING. Discuss with your students the difference between showing and telling, emphasizing the positive impact that showing has on a piece. For example, consider the difference between "It was cold" and "The temperature was four below zero." Give partnered students a set of practice sentences and ask them to move them from a telling statement to a showing statement (Figure 3–12). Bring the group back together to share examples of the enriched sentences. Encourage students to use showing sentences in their writing.

DRAWING FROM WORD LISTS. Encourage the use of interesting words by working with students to develop lists of synonym choices to post and use

Figure 3–12

Change from Telling to Showing	
It was cold.	My desk is messy.
It was hot.	My bedroom is messy.
My mom is nice.	The pizza was good.
My friend is funny.	My sandwich was awful.
The sky was beautiful.	I like school.
The day was dreary.	Recess is fun.
His outfit is colorful.	I am principled.
My bedroom is plain.	I have a good friend.

while writing, for example, *run: scamper, jog, trot, gallop, scurry.* Have them first suggest words spontaneously and then give them time to search books, dictionaries, and thesauri to add to the list. Write the words in alphabetical order so that students can quickly find what they are looking for (or use sticky notes to maintain the ability to move words around). Demonstrate how you use the list while writing.

REWORDING. Show students the process of reading through a current piece you are writing to underline possible words and phrases for rewording. Rewording involves choosing a single word or phrase and replacing it with a more precise or descriptive word or phrase. For example, how many words could be used to describe *get, green, skunk,* or *stinky*? You might need to use a thesaurus. After demonstrating, send students off to reword with a piece of their own writing. Allow students to work with a partner or in teams.

LEARNING FROM PROFESSIONAL AUTHORS. Choose a text in which the author explicitly describes the setting or a character. (See the sidebar for an example of an explicitly described *setting*.) Read the description aloud several times (or project the text), asking students to sketch the image the author creates. Discuss the importance of description in helping develop a piece, and then send students off to

> **A SETTING DESCRIBED**
>
> Nanna and Poppy live in a big house in the middle of town. There's a brick path that goes to the back porch, but before you get there you pass right by the kitchen window.
>
> . . . The kitchen is where Nanna and Poppy are most of the time.
>
> So you can climb on the flower barrel and tap the window. . . .
>
> —Norton Juster,
> *The Hello, Goodbye Window*

develop their own descriptions in the pieces they are working on. After they have had a chance to write, allow students to meet in groups to read their descriptions aloud and have peers sketch. This will help the writers get a feel for whether they have portrayed the intended images.

Using Dialogue

Dialogue is a tool that narrative authors use to move stories along and show how characters respond to and feel about situations. Different types of mini-lessons can be used to teach students to meaningfully incorporate dialogue into their writing. Consider the following:

LEARNING FROM PROFESSIONAL AUTHORS. Show students the use of dialogue in a text that is familiar to them. Discuss how the author uses the dialogue to develop an event and show how characters respond to the situation at hand.

TRYING OUT SPEECH BUBBLES. Sketch an image in relation to the piece you are currently using for demonstration. Use speech bubbles with dialogue to show what the involved people or characters say to one another. Have your students sketch their own moments and use speech bubbles to show the dialogue.

PRACTICING WITH A PAINTING. Have students write dialogue for a painting that features two or more individuals. Show them how to use punctuation to signify the dialogue. The paintings listed in the sidebar (easily located with a Google search) yield some interesting written conversations.

Paintings for Teaching Dialogue

- *The Banjo Lesson*, Henry Ossawa Tanner
- *The Flower Carrier*, Diego Rivera
- *The Giant*, N.C. Wyeth
- *Girls Making Snowman*, Henry Sugimoto
- *The Hairdresser*, Tilly Willis
- *Idylle Enfantine*, William Bouguereau
- *Oh, Yeah*, Norman Rockwell
- *One More Game*, Stephen Scott Young
- *Outward Bound*, Norman Rockwell
- *A Thing About Ice Cream*, Jerome White
- *The Two Fridas*, Frida Kahlo
- *Winter Walk*, Cecil Youngfox

PRACTICING WITH A PICTURE BOOK. Have students write dialogue for one page of a picture book that you have read aloud to them. Show them how to punctuate and use dialogue tags such as *asked*, *answered*, and *shouted*.

WEAVING IN DIALOGUE. Show students how you use dialogue to enrich a narrative you have written. To make your point, start with a dialogue-free text and show how you enhance it by adding dialogue. For example:

Draft 1

We were walking along the path when the dogs disappeared into the brush. Everything seemed to get still and quiet. Karl smelled something. Tomas said it was a skunk.

Draft 2

We were walking along the path when the dogs disappeared into the brush. Everything seemed to get still and quiet.

"Do you smell something," Karl asked?

"Oh, no! Skunnnnk," Tomas shouted!

SCRIPTING COMIC STRIPS. Create a simple three- to six-block comic strip featuring two characters. You can either draw stick characters or use a comic strip creator (see sidebar). Demonstrate how to use speech bubbles, and then partner students to write dialogue and read it aloud to be sure the story works. As an alternative to writing their own language, students may write familiar jokes as a way to develop an understanding of how to organize the dialogue. For example:

Block 1: Knock Knock.

Block 2: Who's there?

Block 3: Little Old Lady.

Block 4: Little Old Lady who?

Block 5: I didn't know you could yodel.

> **COMIC STRIP CREATORS**
> - http://stripgenerator.com/strip/create
> - www.stripcreator.com/make.php#
> - www.makebeliefscomix.com/Comix/

FILLING IN A STORY. Project a comic strip and have students write the story in narrative format. Show them how to keep the dialogue as originally presented, and add description, sensory details, and transition words to create the narrative.

USING DIALOGUE TAGS. Work with students to develop a list of dialogue tags to draw from while writing. Start with a spontaneously generated list. Then give students time to search books and add to the list. Arrange the list alphabetically. This will enable students to quickly check to see if new words are already on the list before adding them. Figure 3–13 shows an example of a class-generated list.

Using Words and Phrases to Signal Event Order

While not the most exciting of all writing concepts to teach, students whose writing has little flow or a mixed-up sequence can generally benefit from lessons focused on using key words and phrases to signal event order.

MAKING THE PROCESS EXPLICIT. Show students a piece of your writing that makes good use of key words and phrases to signal event order. Help them identify key words and their importance to the story. Read and show the story without the words and ask students what impact a lack of such words has on the piece.

LEARNING FROM OTHER STUDENTS. Show students an original draft of a student-written narrative alongside a revised version that has been improved with sequencing words and phrases. Figure 3–14 provides an example from a first-grade student.

Ask students to identify the words and phrases that signify event order. After students examine the samples, work with them to list as many signal words they can think of such as *first, next, last, early, later, the next morning, that evening, when spring arrived*, and so on. Post the list and have them read their own pieces to consider how they might help their audience get a better sense for the flow of events by adding such words and phrases. Keep the list available so that they may add to it as they generate new ideas.

Figure 3–13

Dialogue Tags		
answered	giggled	questioned
asked	hummed	roared
begged	interrupted	said
cried	kidded	screamed
cheered	laughed	sighed
demanded	mumbled	shrugged
exclaimed	murmured	whispered

Figure 3–14

Signal Words in a First-Grade Student's Writing	
Original Draft	**Revised Version**
Me and my mom and dad went to my dance comptishon.	On Saturday me and my mom and dad went to my dance comptishon.
I had butter flys in my stumick	I had butter flys in my stumick befou I went on stage.
I fell.	I fell when I went on stage.
I loved it becos I just got up and ceped dancing.	I loved it becos I just got up and ceped dancing.
Everyone had fun I thinck.	Everyone had fun I thinck.

LEARNING FROM PROFESSIONAL AUTHORS. Provide a structured opportunity for students to learn about sequencing by cutting apart 4–8 key sections of a familiar story and having them put the pieces back together in their original order. Ask them to highlight the words and phrases that signal event order. This is a good opportunity to start (or add to) a class list of sequencing words. Encourage students to use such words in their own writing.

PRACTICE WITH SEQUENCING. Omit the sequencing words from a piece either written by a child or a professionally published author. Have the students add the transitions.

Pacing

Pacing is a narrative technique that authors use to control a reader's movement through a text. Effective pacing serves to maintain the reader's interest and an appropriate sense of suspense; it allows for lingering on details at just the right time and minimizes details at other times. Pacing is a sophisticated technique for the elementary student. Not surprisingly, it doesn't show up in the Common Core standards until grade 5.

WEIGHTING THE IDEAS. To introduce your students to the concept of pacing, chart out the event sequence in a narrative you are using for demonstration and show them how you think through which ideas to elaborate and which to keep minimal or not include at all. Using numbers, give the most "weight" to the events you want to detail and give little or no weight to the events that may not need to be included. An example appears below.

Details	Weight
Picked up friends.	0
Drove to park.	0
Got out and started walking.	1
Dogs got sprayed by skunk.	2
Took dogs home.	1
Called friends' mom.	0
Rinsed dogs with hose.	2
Scrubbed dogs with dog shampoo.	2
Scrubbed dogs with tomato juice.	2
Relaxed after all the activity.	1
Drove friends home.	0

After you model the process, encourage students to chart and weight their own event sequences as appropriate.

EXPLORING PACING TECHNIQUES. After you introduce the concept of pacing give students an overview of techniques they can use to slow or increase the pace. Over time, use your own writing, student samples, and professionally published texts to illustrate the techniques. Figure 3–15 offers a beginning set of techniques.

Figure 3–15

Pacing Techniques	
Techniques for Slowing the Pace	**Techniques for Increasing the Pace**
Provide details about the characters and setting.	Be sparing with details. Focus on what the reader needs to know.
Zoom out and provide broad lens rather than close-up narration.	Zoom in and use close-up narration rather than a broad lens.
Use dialogue that reveals information about the characters and their responses to situations.	Use brief dialogue that moves the plot forward.
Weave in some longer, descriptive sentences (being sure to maintain balance with shorter sentences).	Use mostly short sentences (making sure to maintain some variation in length). Try some sentence fragments.
Use longer paragraphs that include description.	Use short paragraphs.

Crafting a Narrative Text Title

Narrative text without a good title just seems to have something missing, yet students often create the title as a quick afterthought or leave it off altogether. Following are some minilessons designed to support children's consideration and development of rich narrative titles.

PLAYING WITH THREE. Develop three possible titles for a piece you are currently using for demonstration. Ask students which they think works best and why. Send students off to develop three possibilities for the current piece they are writing, and to then work with a partner or team to choose a favorite.

RATIONALIZING A TEXT TITLE. Read a story to the students and don't show or tell the title. Team students to come up with a title possibility that lends insight into some aspect of the content or theme, and then have the larger group vote for the best titles. Discuss why the student-suggested titles work well (or not), and how they compare with the actual text title.

RATIONALIZING TITLE PREFERENCES. Give partnered students a few minutes to choose a favorite title from a narrative text they have read. Ask that they describe *why they like the title* and *how it relates to or enhances the content*. As an alternative to finding great titles, students may find a title in the classroom that doesn't work as well as it could. Have them discuss their rationale for wanting to strengthen it, and suggest a new title.

USING GRAPHIC DESIGN. Choose a piece you are preparing to publish and show students how you use word art (colors, fonts, styles) on the title to reflect the mood and tone of the piece. Give students time to work on their own designs (on the computer or by hand) and describe how they connect with the mood or tone of the piece. Using a computer is ideal because it allows for quick revision and exploration of different looks.

Providing a Sense of Closure

Story language is important right down to the last few words. Therefore, we can't just quickly notify the reader, "That's the end of my story!" Instead, we must offer a sense of closure that brings everything together and sends the reader off with the feeling that the ending was worth reading.

LEARNING FROM PROFESSIONAL AUTHORS. Show the students the endings to a small set of familiar, professionally published narratives and ask what makes them strong or not strong.

TRYING DIFFERENT CLOSURE TECHNIQUES. Review a set of closure techniques, offering examples related to a piece of your own writing. (Figure 3–16 provides an example.) Then, assign students to try three different techniques based on their own pieces and work with a partner or team to select a favorite.

Figure 3–16

Techniques for Closure

- **Scene**: Summarize the ending scene with a visual or sensory image related to the content. ("We all sat down with glasses of water. The dogs were at our feet smelling wet and only a little skunky, and we laughed about our day.")

- **Reaction**: Tell how you feel about the content or share a personal reflection. ("Even after everything that had happened, I was happy with the way the day had turned out.")

- **Statement of personal development**: Tell how you changed as a result of the events described. ("My experiences with these dogs ended up giving me a better sense of humor. I could laugh or cry, and I decided to laugh.")

- **Point for reflection**: End with a statement that encourages readers to keep thinking about the concept at hand. ("So next time you go walking with your dogs. . . .")

- **Audience connection**: Bring the reader into the text. ("So if you go walking your dogs at Hidden Playground Park. . . .")

- **Circle back to the beginning**: Return to the opening image or scene. (The next day we were on the trail again, this time with the dogs on leashes.)

- **Sequel starter**: Set up the reader for a sequel. ("We thought our skunk days were over. Little did we know.")

- **Surprise**: Surprise the reader. ("We sat down with our ice water after this long and adventuresome day. Eventually, the dogs wandered around the house and who should come back clearly having rolled in garbage? You guessed it!")

Collaborative Engagement

To deepen their understanding of key narrative techniques, arrange for students to engage in collaborative analysis and evaluation experiences, peer conferences, and teacher conferences.

Analyzing and Evaluating Writing Samples from the Classroom

After teaching students about the key elements of narrative writing, give groups a sample of student writing (or use teacher writing if you don't yet have a student sample) and ask them to analyze it in light of particular criteria. When working with Anchor 3, select from questions such as those featured in Figure 3–17. After groups meet, you can bring the whole class back together for a follow-up discussion.

Analyzing and Evaluating Mentor Text

An important part of the writing curriculum involves opportunities to read and view text created by professional authors. Using specific questions to analyze the author's craft can open students to new ideas to consider for their own writing.

1. Show students how to reserve a section of the writing notebook to record great ideas or language from the mentor texts. They need not record all of the ideas encountered, but should instead focus on their favorites.

2. After the students read, view, or listen to a text, set them up in groups and give each a copy of the text, directing them to a specific section as appropriate. Assign the groups to work through one to three guiding questions, such as those featured in Figure 3–17. You can differentiate by having different groups work with different questions or texts. Encourage students to jot ideas in their notebooks (or require each student to record at least one idea and share it at the end of the group meeting).

3. Arrange time for the groups to report their findings and observations.

Figure 3–17

Questions for Analyzing and Evaluating Narrative Pieces

Kindergarten

- Who are the characters or people in the piece? How does the illustrator show this?

- How does the author help us get to know the characters?

- What happens? How does the illustrator show this? How does the author show this?

- How does the author feel about what happens? How can you tell?

Grades 1–2

- Who are the characters or people in the piece? How are they introduced?

- What happens? How does the author show this?

- Is there a challenge/goal/problem? What do the characters/people do about it?

- How do they feel about it? How can you tell?

- How did the author close the piece?

Grades 3–5

- How does the author establish the situation? What does the event sequence look like?

- Who does the author have telling the story?

- How does the author use description to develop events or show character views?

- What words are used to help create a picture in the reader's mind?

- How does the author use dialogue to develop events or show character views?

- What words are used to show event order?

- How did the author close the piece?

Grade 5

- What pacing techniques are used? Can we find an example of slow pacing? Can we find an example of quick pacing?

- Find a few short sentences or fragments. What effect do these create? Find a few long sentences. What effect do these create?

Conferring with the Teacher

Conferences are important for all student writers. Conference time may be used to listen to students talk and help them articulate their stories, to teach a specific strategy, or for a quick follow-up to see how newly learned strategies are being incorporated. As a rule of thumb, keep the focus on *teaching the writer* rather than *perfecting the piece*. It can be tempting to help the student create a flawless piece, but it is generally more beneficial to focus on one key concept or strategy that the student can carefully consider and internalize.

When conferring in relation to Anchor 3, keep your focus on Anchor 3 objectives. Organizing the conference with a predictable set of prompts and questions can help students know what to expect and be ready to show you their thinking. See Figure 3–18.

Conferring with Peers

Children can be very capable and responsible responders to their peers' writing, especially when they are given some starting expectations for their conversations. After they have some experience conferring with you, coach them to work in peer conferences or small groups through any of the processes featured in Figure 3–19.

Figure 3–18

Conference Routine

- **Open the conversation**. *How are things going with this piece? Tell me about the story/read this part to me. Is there something you need help with?*

- **Identify notable strengths.** *This part of your drawing helps me picture what happened because. . . . Your introduction draws me in because. . . . I feel like I really understand how the character feels because. . . . Your sequence is well developed because. . . . This closure works so well because. . . . These words seem important because. . . .*

- **Identify one teaching point.** *What do you think you should revise or do next from here? Can you show me how you will start? Or I have one thing I want you to develop and I'm going to help you get started.*

- **Send the student away with something manageable to develop.** *Let's get you started on this and then next time we meet we can talk about how it's going.*

Figure 3–19

Peer Conference Plans

- Ask the author to read the piece with you and tell you about one part he or she likes. Then tell the author about one part that really grabs your attention.

- Tell the author what you feel is a big strength and offer one suggestion. Help the author get started on the suggestion.

- Write a response to the author on a sticky note. Tell one strength you see and offer one suggestion.

- Ask the author to tell you more details about one part of the picture or one part of the story. Help the author with specific ideas to get started on adding details (through drawing, description, or dialogue) about that part, if needed.

- Together with the author, look at our narrative writing checklist (see Figure 3–1) and find all the key parts. Are all the parts present?

- Together with the author, ask, "Does everything make sense?" Help the author get started on fixing any parts that do not make sense.

- Discuss with the author whether attention to pacing might improve the piece. Find one area with either good or poor pacing.

Independent Application

The independent application section offers suggestions for helping students move into different genres of narrative writing. You may cycle back through these applications throughout the year, addressing techniques for revising and editing as described in Sections 4 and 5, bringing in technology as described in Section 6, and teaching research skills as described in Sections 7–9. To introduce each new genre, you may wish to use to the overarching lesson (page 75) as your instructional frame.

Personal Narrative

Personal narratives are first-person stories about events we have experienced in our lives. Usually they involve some sort of goal that is achieved, a tension that is resolved, a challenge that is met, or an event that changes lives. Personal narratives are often written in chronological order and may capture anything from a brief moment in time to a more extended sequence of events. A child might write about how she ended up convincing her mom to make chocolate-chip pancakes for breakfast or about how the bus driver saved a spider's life. She might write about extracting a dime from the tracks of the automatic sliding doors at the grocery store or about the moment she first held her baby sister. Personal narratives are important texts for building familiarity and connections among the children in a classroom. They make excellent material for binding in a class book, creating narrative podcasts (audio or video), or sharing orally.

Memoir

Memoirs are much like personal narratives except that they involve the added element of *looking back and reflecting*. So while a personal narrative tells the story, a memoir also includes commentary on how the events impacted the author's way of being, living in, or viewing the world. Memoirs address some bigger issue about the individual rather than only recounting an experience. For example, while in a personal narrative, a child might tell the story of the moment she first held her baby sister, in memoir she would also include a reflection, such as how from that moment she felt like a more responsible person.

ANCHOR

3

Opportunity to Emphasize
Language Standard 3

> Discuss the use of informal versus formal register. While "voice" is encouraged across text types, personal narratives offer a little more leeway than many other genres.

Testimonio

Testimonio is a literary genre originating in Latin America. Its main purpose is to illuminate the experience of a *people* who have been in some way oppressed or marginalized by telling the story of an *individual*. Students of color, students learning English, immigrant students, or indeed any student whose language, literacy, or life practices have been at some time marginalized may speak through *testimonio*. The experience can be therapeutic and self-empowering.

As with personal narratives and memoirs, *testimonios* describe lived experiences. A unique feature is that they also *connect the story to social, political, or historical conditions that might have impacted the events*. For example, immigrant children might tell the story of coming to the United States, providing commentary on why the move came about. Students learning English as a second language might tell about their experiences negotiating two language systems, providing commentary on the associated social challenges they have encountered with school-based learning. A student who has been the brunt of harmful language or actions by another child might describe the experience, and provide commentary on family, peer, or school factors associated with bullying. By design and intention, *testimonio* can raise awareness of the life experience of children who have been marginalized, and engage them in the political act of "remembering" (Saavedra 2011).

Oral History

Opportunity to Emphasize
Language Standard 3

❯ Show students how to capture the actual language that was used in the interview response, which is likely to be informal. Contrast this with the more formal narrative that will be used for the write-up. Maintaining the speaker's voice enhances the richness of oral history pieces.

Oral histories are stories about events in other people's lives, primarily collected through interviewing. The interviews may take place in person, by phone, by email, or through a video communication service (such as Skype). Elementary-aged students often interview a grandparent or an older relative—someone with whom they feel comfortable communicating. A family member can help do the recording of responses. Interview responses are contextualized with narrative, and arranged and sequenced in such a way that they may be logically understood and preserved for future generations.

Figure 3–20 provides examples of the types of questions that oral historians ask. You may use this list as a starting point, but your students are most likely to become invested if they take part in choosing and developing the questions.

Biography

A good biography tells the story of another person's life and helps the reader understand the historical context in which that life was lived. Help students understand that biographies are made up of a series of ministories. Students

Figure 3–20

Questions for Oral Histories

1. What has been the most important world event in your lifetime?

2. Where did you grow up? Tell me about your childhood home(s) and neighborhood(s).

3. What languages were spoken in your childhood home and neighborhood?

4. Tell me about your elementary school(s). What teachers do you remember? How did you get to school? What did you eat there?

5. What did you play when you were a child? With whom did you play?

6. What stories do you remember hearing about yourself when you were little?

7. What stories have your families passed on to you?

8. What do you remember about your grandparents? What stories did they tell you?

can get their information for biographies either by interviewing both their subjects and subjects' acquaintances and/or by reading literature focused on the individual. A timeline can be used for planning, or students may write one event per page, and then organize their pages in some meaningful order. (Biographies are not always presented in time order. For example, they may begin in the present; or, they may include flashbacks.) K–2 students typically choose *someone they know* while students in grades 3 to 5 often research *someone in the public eye*—a current or historic figure.

Narrative Fiction

Narrative fiction is often presented in the form of a story book. Students may write stories in the form of realistic fiction, historic fiction, mystery, folktales, fantasy, fables, and/or other genres. Such stories generally contain a plot and often a theme.

- **Realistic fiction:** Plots address everyday events and relationships from contemporary times; they may be framed as a mystery, survival story, drama, or humorous piece.

- **Historical fiction:** Plots are developed out of a realistic portrayal of a historic period; they address everyday events of the times and reflect experiences and social relationships as they were influenced by cultural norms of the time.

- **Folktales:** Plots portray the adventures of human or animal characters learning lessons; they often involve supernatural antagonists such as trolls and witches. Folktales are often set in the past; conflict between good and evil is typical.

- **Fantasy:** Plots portray believable stories with elements of reality altered; they often have universal themes (good vs. evil); and often involve outlandish characters or settings.

- **Fables:** Plots portray the experiences of animal characters who learn a lesson through their behaviors; the animals have obvious human characteristics such as "silly," "kind," "sly," or "lazy."

- **Myths:** Content may include humans or supernatural heroes or deities. Myths were once considered legitimate explanations for questions of life and cultural practices, such why the sun travels across the sky; why it thunders; why there is morning dew; why it is wise to avoid habits such as acting with arrogance or divulging secrets.

PRODUCTION AND DISTRIBUTION OF WRITING

English Language Arts Standards: Writing ANCHOR 4

Writing Anchor 4: Produce clear and coherent writing in which the development, organization, and style are appropriate to task, purpose, and audience.

Kindergarten	First	Second	Third	Fourth	Fifth
Begins in grade 3.	Begins in grade 3.	Begins in grade 3.	With guidance and support from adults, produce writing in which the development and organization are appropriate to task and purpose. (Grade-specific expectations for writing types are defined in standards 1–3.)	Produce clear and coherent writing in which the development and organization are appropriate to task, purpose, and audience. (Grade-specific expectations for writing types are defined in standards 1–3.)	Produce clear and coherent writing in which the development and organization are appropriate to task, purpose, and audience. (Grade-specific expectations for writing types are defined in standards 1–3.)

Although the Common Core State Standards do not list specific expectations for Anchor 4 until grade 3, K–2 teachers should consider the lessons in this section, as they provide building blocks for the work of students in grades 3–5. Work toward Anchor 4 is relevant for students in all grades.

Decision Tree for **Writing** ANCHOR 4

> ## Is now a good time for focused instruction in relation to Writing Anchor 4?
>
> Anchor 4 requires that students *produce clear and coherent writing in which the development, organization, and style are appropriate to task, purpose, and audience.* To support your students in developing skill in this area, it is recommended that you implement three types of instruction:
>
> | Demonstration | Collaborative Engagement | Independent Application |
> |:---:|:---:|:---:|
> | Page 111 | Page 130 | Page 133 |
>
> An initial overarching demonstration occurs first, followed by a formative assessment. After analyzing the assessment data, you can use the information below to plan your subsequent instruction, considering whether to implement the lessons with the whole class or small groups.

Minilessons

After assessing your students' work with any text type from Section 1, 2, or 3, choose from the following based on their needs:

Clarity and Coherence

- Rereading (page 116)
- Staying on Topic (page 116)
- Including Everything Important (page 117)
- Weeding Out the Unimportant (page 118)
- Attending to Sentence Order (page 118)
- Attending to Sentence Content (page 119)
- Paragraphing (page 120)

Appropriateness to Task, Purpose, and Audience

- Choosing Appropriate Content (page 122)
- Choosing Appropriate Formats and Media (page 123)
- Attending to Voice (page 124)
- Merging Attention to Role, Audience, Format, and Topic (RAFT) (page 128)

Collaborative Engagement

Use the following experiences to encourage deeper consideration of key writing concepts:

- Analyzing and Evaluating Writing Samples from the Classroom (page 130)
- Conferring with the Teacher (page 130)
- Conferring with Peers (page 131)

Independent Application

Anchor 4 competencies are applied to the independent application experiences described in Sections 1–3. No new applications (text types/genres) are described for Anchor 4. The lessons should be implemented after particular types/genres have been taught. The focus is on fine-tuning and revising pieces to ready them for production and distribution. Anchor 4 is the first of the standards within the *Production and Distribution of Writing* category.

Demonstration

Anchor 4 requires that students *produce clear and coherent writing in which the development, organization, and style are appropriate to task, purpose, and audience*. This is the first of the standards within the *Production and Distribution of Writing* category, and as such it involves a shift from planning and drafting with structure in mind to an *additional* focus on fine-tuning and revising with the audience's experience in mind. One part of the focus involves meeting the content and structural expectations of Anchors 1 to 3. Whether writing an argument, an informational text, or a narrative, the basic elements of content and structure must be in place. But with Anchor 4, there's something more: students must also attend to fine-tuning their work in ways that make it *clear, coherent*, and *just right* for the reader.

Clear and coherent writing stays on topic and reads smoothly. The audience doesn't get stuck wondering what the author is trying to say or where the content is going—and the piece sounds good when it is read aloud. *Just-right* writing is tailored to the specific task, purpose, and audience. It is enriched beyond generic structural requirements with thoughtfully selected content and formatting, and with a voice that engages the reader and makes the piece come to life.

Achieving Anchor 4 expectations is a tall order for elementary students, so it makes sense that it is not until grade 3 that the Common Core defines grade-specific requirements for this standard. But attention to Anchor 4 must not be absent in the K–2 classroom. To ensure a steady flow of development, K–2 students should begin to attend to issues of clarity, coherence, and appropriateness to ease the transition into grade 3.

Overarching Lesson

To prepare for this lesson, be ready to demonstrate writing and revising within a text type you have already taught (see Sections 1–3). (Leave areas that need revision.) Rather than using the lesson to be explicit about text type (as with Anchors 1–3), your explicit focus will be on demonstrating an effort toward clear and coherent writing that is styled just right for a rich audience experience.

1. **Purpose**

   - Tell students that now that they know what to include with (an opinion piece/an informational text/a narrative), you will be showing them how to think in additional ways about meeting the needs of their audience.

   - Tell them that after your demonstration they will be considering the concepts you are discussing in light of their current pieces.

2. **Expectations.** Briefly show students the expectations for Anchor 4 at your grade level (Figure 4–1) and let them know that these are concepts they should be considering with every piece they write for publication.

3. **Demonstration.** Working with a draft you already have going, show students how you review it for clarity, coherence, and appropriateness. Specifically:

   - Is this going to make sense when someone else reads it?

   - Is the information organized in the best way possible?

   - Does it have everything it needs?

   - Is it right for this audience?

   - How do I sound?

   The general method for this overarching lesson is to reread, changing or marking parts to work toward clarity, coherence, and tailoring to achieve the author's intended goals. With students in kindergarten and first grade, this may involve erasing certain words and adding others, while students moving through grades can be expected to produce more than one draft.

FOR ENGLISH LEARNERS

Students learning English do not need to wait for full competency in English before they can work toward clear and coherent writing appropriate to task, purpose, and audience. In fact, working in this direction will support their English learning and will strengthen their writing. Consider the following:

- Have the student draw before writing to create a visual context for discussing the content. During the discussion, guide the student to jot down key vocabulary and syntax (or sentences) that will support the writing.

- Listen to students read their writing and help them identify parts they think could use revision. Help them to revise toward correct or more complex syntax and vocabulary.

- After students have revised a piece or section with your support, read their writing aloud to them and have them repeat after you so that they develop a feel for the flow of the language. The goal is not so much to develop pronunciation as it is to develop a sense of English syntax that will support future writing.

4. **Student Writing**

- As students move to their writing, encourage revision toward a clear and coherent piece that does just what they intend and sounds just right.

- Arrange adequate time for students to write. Let them know that you will be using their pieces to inform your next steps in instruction.

5. **Assessment.** Collect each student's writing to determine how well your class is meeting the expectations for Anchor 4. Using a class record (Figure 4–2) will offer an overview of what the class needs and will show individual students' growth from a pre- to a postassessment.

Using Assessment to Inform Instruction

To continue your instruction after the initial assessment, plan to support students in revising their current pieces. If the class record (Figure 4–2) shows that most students could use instruction in a particular area, it is advisable to keep the class together for the minilessons. If the record shows varied needs, then provide a mix of minilessons, pulling students in to work with you depending on the needs they have demonstrated. The decision tree on page 110 can help you to set your course.

Figure 4–1

CHECKLIST OF EXPECTATIONS
FOR WRITING ANCHOR 4

Grades K–2

❏ Standards for Anchor 4 begin in grade 3.

Grade 3

❏ Development and organization are appropriate to task and purpose.

Grade 4

❏ Produces clear and coherent writing.

❏ Development and organization are appropriate to task, purpose, and audience.

Grade 5

❏ Produces clear and coherent writing.

❏ Development and organization are appropriate to task, purpose, and audience.

Although the Common Core document does not list specific expectations for Anchor 4 until grade 3, K–2 teachers should consider the lessons in this section, as they provide building blocks for the work of students in grades 3–5.

ANCHOR

4

Figure 4–2

Class Record for Anchor 4: Grades 3–5

Student Names	Grade-Level Expectations					
	Writing is clear and coherent.		Content and format are appropriate to task, purpose, and audience.		Voice and style are appropriate to task, purpose, and audience.	
	Date	Date	Date	Date	Date	Date

0 = Not Present   1 = Could Use Development   2 = Developed

ANCHOR

4

Minilessons: Clarity and Coherence

Rereading

Rereading is a first step in learning to revise toward clarity and coherence and should be developed as a habit as early as kindergarten. Children who develop the habit of rereading—even when they have written just a sentence or two—often notice errors, word omissions, and missing information, and can be encouraged to quickly fix this by erasing, crossing off, or adding text. The minilessons below take revision into more depth, but a habit of rereading serves as the basis for all. Regularly show students how you reread your own writing, fixing things as you go.

Staying on Topic

Staying on topic is the ultimate tactic for achieving clarity and coherence. If you have students who need work in this area, show them how to revise a piece that veers off topic. You may use a piece of your own writing or a piece of student writing. A student example appears below.

1. Let students know that they will be reading a piece that has some good content but goes off topic and therefore does not completely do the job the author set out to do.

   ### Responsibility Narrative

   A time when I was responsibile was when I got my cat Lilac. I feed her, I always play with her and I do her litter. Let's just say it sitinks. It smells terrible but I LOVE love love love love her ever so much! She sort of looks like the lion in the wizard of oz because she is vary fluffy. She is grey. Her full name is Lilac of Spring. She sleeps in our geroge. In the winter she sleeps inside. She is the best cat I could ever have. I love her so much! And that is how I am responsibile.

2. Read together through the piece one time to identify what the author seemed to intend as the focus. (Or you can tell the students the intended focus beforehand.)

3. Read back through the piece and highlight parts that could be removed because they veer off topic.

4. Now that the off-topic parts have been separated, discuss what the author could do to round out the piece with relevant information.

For example, the student might develop each of the three acts of responsibility that are mentioned (feeding, playing, and litter).

5. Arrange for students to use highlighters to help evaluate the organization and focus of their current pieces.

Including Everything Important

Just as it is important to stay on topic, another key element of working toward coherence is ensuring that all of the important details that carry a sequence are in place.

1. To emphasize the importance of details, construct a piece in which something important is left out, or use a well-chosen student sample. A teacher sample appears below, with information missing after the third paragraph.

Mouse Trouble

What a fun field trip! We had just completed the farm tour. Our last stop was the cow pasture. While counting heads so we could get back on the bus, I felt a mouse run up my pant leg . . . all the way to the knee. "Don't scream," I urged myself. "You are a role model for these children." I bent down and cupped the mouse from outside my pants.

The nearest building was the farmhouse. Still cupping the mouse I hobble-sprinted to it, pushed open the door, found a bedroom, and locked myself inside. I couldn't move.

There was a knock at the door. "Ma'am? Is everything all right?" I recognized the farmer's voice. "Everything's fine!" I broke into a sweat. "But there's a mouse in my pants."

When I came out of the farmhouse, the children had loaded the bus. The parents looked at me questioningly. I just shook my head.

2. Read the piece aloud and ask students whether anything seems to be missing. With their help, think aloud about what a reader would still want to know, and jot down where you will put the additional information.

3. After the demonstration, provide an opportunity for peers to work together to help identify whether anything seems missing in a partner's piece. The goal is to ensure that the audience will not be left with questions.

Weeding Out the Unimportant

Sometimes students can move a piece closer to coherence by weeding out little bits of *extra* or *unimportant* information.

1. Type up a piece or section of your own writing or student writing containing sentences and/or phrases that could be removed with the intention of strengthening the piece. Challenge students to highlight the parts that could be removed. An example (personal narrative) from a student appears below.

The Hot Sail

It was the hottest sailing day of the year. The air was as humid as steam. I had on a swimsuit and a hot and sweaty life jacket. The sun burned my legs. Even the weeds in the water seemed warm. There are so many weeds because grass chemicals from yards go into the lake and make more weeds grow.

Being out on the water didn't help with the heat. Every time I put my foot in the lake it kept drying up right away. My dad won't let me put anything more than a foot in the lake when we are sailing, and actually it's hard to convince him that even a foot is okay.

Finally, after sailing for hours mostly on the north end of the lake, we came close to the shore. My mom and I were so sweaty we were relieved to jump off the boat before it reached the shore. We swam toward the docks. On the way, we saw a funny looking seagull. When we reached the dock we just stayed there for a couple minutes. My poor dad had to get to the shore and take the sail down all by himself.

2. After students highlight parts for removal, have them read the piece both ways (with and without the removed parts) to be sure they like their choices.

3. After practicing on a sample, encourage students to return to their own pieces and highlight extras that might be removed.

Attending to Sentence Order

When students are writing, their sentences don't always emerge in an order that ultimately makes sense for presentation. The result is often a piece full of good ideas that are in a mixed-up order. Learning to revise sentence order—and filling in where connections are missing—is an important skill. Two possibilities follow.

USE EVERY OTHER LINE. Show students how to write on every other line so if necessary they can cut apart sentences and reorder them, removing sentences if needed and filling in ideas on additional paper or sticky notes to create a meaningful whole. (Even if they don't cut, having a little extra writing space on the paper can be helpful for filling in ideas.) Using a word processor is another way to revise order, but students often find it easier to move around and play with concrete parts they can easily and quickly manipulate.

NUMBER THE SENTENCES. Show students how to go through and number their sentences in an order that would work better than the current order. If a key piece of information is missing, it can be written on a sticky note and labeled with a *point five* (as in *1.5*) to show where it should fall. The piece should then be read through before a fresh draft is produced to be sure the new order works.

Attending to Sentence Content

Along with sentence order, sentence content can affect clarity and coherence. If you have students who tend to write with either long or choppy sentences, minilessons focused on *sentence dividing* or *sentence combining* may be of use.

SENTENCE DIVIDING. Some students have a tendency to write very long sentences with lots of ideas or "thought units" that would be better separated into two or more parts. Readers intuitively expect a signal to pause and process, and a sentence provides that signal. Show students how to look for sentences in their work that have too many units for a reader to process at once, and how they might divide the sentence into meaningful parts. When seeking a division point, it can be helpful to look for commas (assuming the student has used commas), and it also can help to look for words such as *and*, *then*, *but*, *so*, and *which*. You may demonstrate the process using anonymous student work or a practice piece created just for the purpose of this exercise. An example follows:

> When we play spy, my mom is usually going through recipes or reading in the living room and we go around behind her or sneak in front of her and try to stay hidden but if someone makes a sound or if she sees someone, she tells us and then we start over again.

SENTENCE COMBINING. An issue similar to students writing too-long sentences is students writing too many too-short or "choppy" sentences. Short sentences can be an excellent tool for effect. They can help emphasize a point

> **Opportunity to Emphasize**
> **Language Standard 1**
>
> ❯ Discuss how to create, expand, and punctuate a variety of sentence types.
>
> ❯ Recognize ineffective sentences and learn strategies for improving them.

or pick up the pace of a narrative. But they often work best when intermingled with other sentences that vary in length. Show students the appeal of such variation by sharing a choppy piece and then challenging them to help you improve it by combining some of the sentences. A practice piece follows:

Short and choppy: Reagan and I walked down the dock. A ladder was at the end. We each went down one step. The water was freezing. We each came back out. I wanted to jump in. Reagan didn't want to. I said we should jump. I finally jumped in.

Varied Lengths: Reagan and I walked down the dock to the ladder at the end. We each went down one step but the water was freezing. We each came back out. I wanted to jump in. Reagan didn't want to. I said, "Reagan, let's jump!" I finally jumped in.

While the short and choppy version is not necessarily weak, the combined thought units in the second piece give it an easier flow and a more mature feel. After students have seen you working with sentences—whether to divide or combine—they can be encouraged to consider appropriate variation in their own writing.

Paragraphing

As elementary students begin to write pieces that contain more than a few sentences, paragraphing becomes an important tool. Paragraphing can help with clarity and coherence and ultimately helps shape a writer's meaning by giving cues that something new is being introduced or something is about to change. Consider the following minilessons.

IDENTIFYING THE USES OF A PARAGRAPH. Discuss with the students the role of the paragraph in writing and work together to generate a list of tips for when to consider one. For example, a paragraph might be used to do the following:

- Open a piece.
- Close a piece.
- Start a new topic.
- Give a new example.
- Give a new reason.
- Introduce a new character or scene.
- Change the time or setting.
- Indicate a new speaker when dialogue is being used.

After creating the list with your students, make it available for them as they write and revise, and encourage them to reference it during peer and teacher conferences.

PARAGRAPH LOCATING. Select a piece of your own or student writing that needs work with paragraphing. Project the piece or give copies to partners or small groups. Ask students to indicate where paragraphs might logically begin and articulate how their suggestions will enhance clarity, coherence, or meaning.

PARAGRAPH DIVIDING. Find a piece of well-written literature from some area of the curriculum and select four or five paragraphs to use for study. Type the piece onto one page, removing the paragraphs. Place students with partners and tell them the number of paragraphs the piece should contain. Have them find the best possible division using the number you have given. Then show how the author divided the paragraphs and discuss the possible reasons for doing so.

Minilessons: Appropriateness to Task, Purpose, and Audience

While there is not always a clear separation between *clarity and coherence*, and *appropriateness to task, purpose, and audience*, the minilessons in the previous section are focused mostly on clarity and coherence, and the minilessons in the present section focus mostly on appropriateness. This section moves away from the focus on making sure things make sense to a focus on making sure the content, format, and use of language are just right for the piece at hand.

Choosing Appropriate Content

A key goal of Anchor 4 is to get students working toward content that is appropriate to task, purpose, and audience. Achieving appropriateness requires keeping the material engaging and at the interest level of the audience; and it is about knowing what *not* to include. To illustrate the concept of appropriateness, show a map with information that might be included in a piece of writing you are using for demonstration. Along with some genuinely interesting ideas, include a piece of information that is likely to be uninteresting or too obvious for the intended audience. An example from a teacher working with upper elementary students writing for a K–1 audience appears below.

Show how you think through the appropriateness of your content by asking a routine set of questions:

- What would be interesting for this audience?
- What is too tedious or obvious?

Writing for a K–1 audience, five of the six bubbles would probably be informative and interesting, while one would feel kind of obvious. (The *Four Legs* bubble would be more appropriate in a piece written for a two- or three-year-old audience.) Cross off the information that is not appropriate to include. Students can use this same process of consideration with all kinds of writing—whether using a map (as in the example) or working directly on a draft.

Choosing Appropriate Formats and Media

Formatting can make or break a piece. When the content of a long stretch of text could have been presented as a list or graph, when there are no headers or sections, or when key information is buried within the text without bolded fonts or any such variation, the piece can lose appeal. During the elementary years, students can learn to use appropriate formats and media to make their content clear, coherent, and appropriate to task, purpose, and purpose. The sidebar features some examples.

1. To help your students understand different formatting options, lay out a set of informational texts and allow partnered students to choose one. The books should focus on familiar content so that students will be able to understand the connection between the narrative and the formatting/media choices the author has selected.

2. Ask the students to purposefully locate interesting uses of formatting/media, and report them back to groups or the class, describing

FORMATTING AND MEDIA FOR ENRICHING A TEXT

Bulleted lists	Labels	Boxes
Numbered lists	Captions	Headers
Charts	Photographs	Fonts
Webs	Drawings	Word art
Graphs	Clip art	Shading
Maps	Sideboxes	Icons

their use. Use the opportunity to make a class list of formatting possibilities (such as the one above) that you and the students can refer back to over time.

3. Over time, show students how you use different formats and media in your own pieces. If you are writing in the same genres as your students, they will likely find opportunities to explore the possibilities you are demonstrating. For example, if everyone is writing a recipe, show how you use numbered lists and formatting on the page to aid in coherence; if everyone is writing all-about books, demonstrate how you use headers to categorize information, charts and tables to condense information, and a bold font for key words. As appropriate, show students how an explanation in the narrative is sometimes necessary for interpreting or drawing the reader's attention to special features such as charts or tables.

Attending to Voice

Along with appropriate content and format, *voice* is critical for connecting with the audience. Voice is the "person" in the piece (Graves 1983). It is that special something that sets the mood and tone and brings a composition to life through the individuality of the writer. Writers have many voices, which they learn to tailor to task, purpose, and audience. Children must learn to summon the voice that is most appropriate for the piece at hand (Culham 2003).

READING AND LISTENING. One way for students to learn about voice is to read and listen to well-crafted texts, giving special consideration to how the author sounds and uses language in unique ways. Figure 4–3 offers a set of recommended texts. To encourage a developing understanding of voice as you read and discuss these texts with students, offer prompts such as the following:

• Listen to how this writer sounds. What do you notice? Why do you think the author chose this style?

• Can you sense that there is a person on the other end of the words? How? What gives this writing a personal touch?

• Can you tell the author cares about the topic? Can you tell the author has an interest in crafting language?

• Do you feel a tone, such as gentleness, playfulness, affection, warmth, friendliness, peacefulness, humor, or sarcasm?

• Is there a way to tell it's "this" author and not another? What stands out?

Figure 4–3

Mentor Texts for Exploration of Voice

Literature/Narrative	
Brown Bear, Brown Bear, What Do You See? Bill Martin Jr.	Purple Cat, Purple Cat, What do you see? I see a white dog looking at me.
Kitten's First Full Moon, Kevin Henkes	It was Kitten's first full moon. When she saw it, she thought. There's a little bowl of milk in the sky. And she wanted it.
Diary of a Worm, Doreen Cronin	I got into a fight with Spider today. He told me you need legs to be cool. Then he ran. I couldn't keep up. Maybe he's right.
Wilfrid Gordon McDonald Partridge, Mem Fox	There was once a small boy called Wilfrid Gordon McDonald Partridge and what's more he wasn't very old, either. His house was next door to an old people's home and he knew all the people who lived there. . . .
The Other Side, Jacqueline Woodson	That summer there was a girl who wore a pink sweater. Each morning she climbed up on the fence and stared over at our side. Sometimes I stared back. She never sat on that fence with anybody, that girl didn't.
The Table Where Rich People Sit, Byrd Baylor	If you could see us sitting here at our old, scratched-up kitchen table, you'd know that we aren't rich.
The True Story of the 3 Little Pigs, Jon Scieszka	Everybody knows the story of the Three Little Pigs. Or at least they think they do. But I'll let you in on a little secret. Nobody knows the real story, because nobody has ever heard *my* side of the story.
John Henry, Julius Lester	You have probably never heard of John Henry. Or maybe you heard about him but don't know the ins and outs of his comings and goings. Well that's why I'm going to tell you about him.

(continues)

Figure 4–3 (*continued*)

Mentor Texts for Exploration of Voice

Informational	
What Is an Amphibian? Feana Tu'akoi	If it has webbed feet, it is an amphibian. Not always. . . . Most amphibians **do** have webbed feet, but so do ducks, pelicans and otters, and they are not amphibians.
Follow the Water from Brook to Ocean, Arthur Dorros	After the next big rain storm, put your boots on and go outside. Look at the water dripping from your roof. Watch it gush out of the drainpipes. You can see water flowing down your street, too.
Germs! Germs! Germs! Bobbi Katz	Food-Put Awayers! Another bad bunch! They won't let us grow in your supper or lunch. Into the fridge go milk, butter, and meat. How can we get into the food that you eat?
How People Learned to Fly, Fran Hodgkins and True Kelley	When you see a bird flying, do you dream about flying too? Do you run with your arms out, imagining that you're soaring among the clouds? Do you make paper airplanes? Do you fly kites?
Poop: A Natural History of the Unmentionable, Nicola Davies	Poop, big jobs, number two. Whatever you call it, feces (to give it one of its proper names) are everywhere. We humans may find it revolting, but the truth is that just about every animal poops.
Throw Your Tooth on the Roof: Tooth Traditions Around the World, Selby Beeler	Has this ever happened to you? You find a loose tooth in your mouth. Yikes! You can wiggle it with your finger. You can push it back and forth with your tongue. Then one day it falls out.
The Journey: Stories of Migration, Cynthia Rylant	The wings of a butterfly seem so delicate that it is hard to imagine this fragile insect traveling much farther than from flower to flower. But one beautiful butterfly—the monarch butterfly—is stronger than it looks.
A River Ran Wild, Lynne Cherry	Long ago a river ran wild through a land of towering forests. Bears, moose, and herds of deer, hawks and owls all made their homes in the peaceful river valley.

STUDYING DIFFERENT VOICES ON THE SAME TOPIC. Gather two or three texts focused on the same topic. For example, you might use an informational trade book, a poem, and a piece from an encyclopedia—all focused on a single topic such as *mice*, *snakes*, *rain*, or *friendship*. Read aloud a portion of each text and discuss the different ways the authors sound as they address the topic. Discuss with students how they want to sound with the current pieces they are writing.

ADDING VOICE. Look through the texts in your classroom and find one that feels devoid of voice. Give student partners or teams a paragraph from the text and ask them to rewrite it to give it voice. Students then read both pieces aloud as a way to understand the contrast (Culham 2005). As an option, you can *assign* a voice for different groups to try. For example, how would the text be different if written by the president or a favorite singer on the pop charts or the principal of the school?

REMOVING VOICE. Just as students can work to add voice to a piece, they can work to remove it. Give students a section of professionally published text rich in voice and ask them to make it dull or sterile. Removing voice is a way to build student understanding of its value (Culham 2005).

PRACTICE MATCHING VOICE WITH TASK, PURPOSE, AND AUDIENCE. Anchor 4 is concerned with appropriateness to task, purpose, and audience. This mini-lesson is designed to draw student attention to all three.

1. Give partnered students three slips of paper, one indicating a task, one indicating a purpose, and one indicating an audience. Figure 4–4 provides a set of slips that may be cut up and used for this purpose. For example, students might end up with the following:

   - *Task*: write an email

   - *Purpose*: to complain to

   - *Audience*: a favorite author

2. Partnered students complete the task as designated on the slips. You may wish to give a time or length limit since this is a practice experience rather than an authentic writing experience.

3. Guide the larger group to discuss the different voices that emerge in the pieces, focusing attention on how task, purpose, and audience affect voice.

Opportunity to Emphasize
Language Standard 3

❯ Compare formal and informal uses of language as they appear in different text types and genres.

ANCHOR

4

Figure 4–4

Task	Purpose	Audience
Write a voice mail message	to thank	a favorite author
Write a text message	to request information from	a friend
Write an email	to request an action by	a teacher
Write a Facebook message	to offer something to	kindergarten students
Write a letter	to express approval to	fifth-grade students
Write a radio announcement	to invite	the principal
Write a television announcement	to apologize to	the community
Write a billboard message	to complain to	the president

Merging Attention to Role, Audience, Format, and Topic (RAFT)

RAFT (adapted from Adler 1989) is a widely used writing strategy that helps students reflect on their voices as writers in light of *audience*, *format*, and *topic*. To prepare for this lesson, decide on the genre/format (as described in Sections 1 to 3) and topic area you want your students to work in for this piece. You will be modeling the use of RAFT to shape a piece within the chosen genre. For example, if your class is engaged in a study of sharing the planet, and each student is writing about an animal, you might use the following:

> *Role*: Animal living in a forest
>
> *Audience*: Farmer needing cleared land
>
> *Format*: Persuasive letter
>
> *Topic*: Deforestation

1. Demonstrate the process of defining each RAFT element listed in Figure 4–5 in light of your chosen content. You should write out your role, audience, format, and topic, and list your plan for each.

2. After laying out your RAFT, send students off to define each RAFT element for their own piece. It is recommended that you use a familiar format or genre so that students can gain experience writing within it—or assign the format/genre with the intention of providing instruction in relation to structure (Anchors 1–3) as you implement the lesson. Provide support as students define their elements.

Figure 4–5

RAFT Writing Strategy

ROLE: **Who am I as I write this piece?**

Examples: a famous person in history; an animal on the endangered species list; a sports referee; an expert on watching little brothers; a child with important ideas; a rabbit character who learns a lesson; a character from a favorite book.

AUDIENCE: **Who am I writing for?**

Examples: younger students who want to learn about my topic; other students in my class; kids who are looking to be entertained; the readership of the school newspaper; a company or business; a favorite author; all people living in the United States.

FORMAT: **What format (genre) am I using?**

Examples: book review; biography; informational article; personal narrative; folktale; informational web page (see Figure 4–9 for a list of possibilities).

TOPIC: **What am I writing about?**

Examples: water pollution; recess; North Atlantic whales; a favorite book; good sportsmanship; a day in the life of someone or something.

3. Pull the students back together. Using guidelines for writing your chosen text type (see Anchor 1, 2, or 3), either talk through what you would include in the piece or demonstrate laying out the ideas in writing as the students observe.

4. Send students off to write their own pieces.

5. Provide structured opportunities for students to share their work and discuss the voices that have emerged in the pieces.

Collaborative Engagement

To deepen their understanding of key concepts related to Anchor 4, arrange for students to engage in collaborative analysis and evaluation experiences, peer conferences, and teacher conferences.

Analyzing and Evaluating Writing Samples from the Classroom

After students have worked with you to develop understandings about clarity, coherence, and appropriateness, give small groups a sample of student writing (or use teacher writing if you don't yet have a student sample) and ask them to analyze it in light of particular criteria. When working with Anchor 4, select from questions such as those featured in Figure 4–6.

Conferring with the Teacher

Conferences are an excellent forum for supporting revision. Conference time may be used to discuss issues of clarity and coherence, to teach a specific strategy for enhancing content or formatting, or for a quick follow-up to see how newly learned strategies are being incorporated. As a rule of thumb, keep the focus on *teaching the writer* rather than *perfecting the piece*. It can be

Figure 4–6

Questions for Evaluating Student Samples in Relation to Anchor 4

- Which parts of the piece do you find most interesting? (Students may underline interesting parts or mark them with a check mark or small sticky note.)

- Are there parts you find too obvious or tedious? (Students may put a squiggly line under parts they would weed out or remove.)

- Do you find yourself confused in any place? (Students may highlight confusing parts or mark them with a star or small sticky note). How might you fix that?

- How is the pacing?

- Does the sentence order seem right? (Students may suggest a new sequence by numbering.)

- How is the sentence variation?

- What types of formatting/media are used to share different kinds of information (as in headers, bulleted lists, captions, graphs, maps, and so on)? Is there any part that might work better if different formatting were used?

- Find a line or section where the author's voice really stands out as appropriate to the piece. What do you think of the voice used for this piece? Why?

tempting to help the student create a flawless piece, but it is generally more beneficial to focus on one key concept or strategy that the student can carefully consider and internalize.

When working with English learners, keep your conference focus just a step ahead of the student's current level of development. Correcting an entire piece so that it reads perfectly in English may not be as powerful as sitting together with the student to work on a specific competency such as choosing precise vocabulary or acceptable syntax or constructing the language for a set of topic sentences. We want students to be able to internalize what we are teaching, and internalization happens when the instruction is comprehensible.

When conferring in relation to Anchor 4, keep your focus on Anchor 4 objectives. Organizing the conference with a predictable set of prompts and questions can help students know what to expect and be ready to show you their thinking. See Figure 4–7.

Conferring with Peers

Children can be very capable and responsible responders to their peers' writing, especially when they are given some starting expectations for their conversations. After they have some experience conferring with you, coach them to work in peer conferences or small groups through any of the processes featured in Figure 4–8. You may wish to occasionally allow students to invite a peer to revision conferences to help both prepare for collaboration.

Figure 4–7

Conference Routine

- **Open the conversation**. *How are things going with this piece? Tell me about it/ read this part to me. Is there something you need help with?*

- **Identify notable strengths.** *These sentences hum right along. . . . Listen to how this part stays right on topic. . . . I really think an audience would be interested in this part. . . . Your voice/the character's voice really captures me here because. . . .*

- **Identify one teaching point.** *Think about (clarity, coherence, voice, content, sentencing, formatting). What do you think you should revise or do next from here? Can you show me how you will start? Or I have one thing I want you to try/develop and I'm going to help you get started working on it.*

- **Send the student away with something manageable to develop.** *Let's get you started on this and then next time we meet we can talk about how it's going.*

Figure 4–8

Peer Conference Plans

- Together with the author, ask: Does everything make sense? Help the author get started on fixing any parts that do not make sense.

- Together with the author, ask: Does the piece stay on topic? Help the author get started on fixing any parts that do not stay on topic.

- Together with the author, look for variety in sentence lengths. Is there a good mix? Find the longest sentence. Is it too long?

- Listen to the author read the text aloud. Together, discuss "What would the audience find most interesting? What else would the audience want to know? Does any of this seem too obvious or unimportant to include?"

- Listen to the author read the text aloud. Afterward, talk about the use of formatting/media. Talk about why each feature was used and whether anything needs development or clarification.

- Listen to the author read the text aloud. Afterward, point out what makes this piece sparkle in terms of voice.

Independent Application

For independent application, students are expected to apply the concepts taught through Anchor 4 minilessons to the types of writing emphasized in Sections 1–3, as shown in Figure 4–9.

Figure 4–9

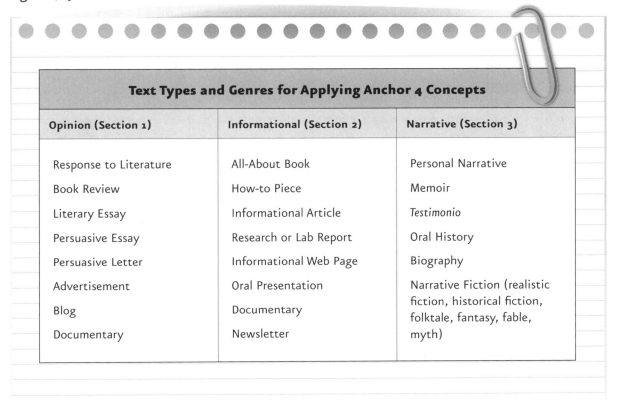

Text Types and Genres for Applying Anchor 4 Concepts		
Opinion (Section 1)	**Informational (Section 2)**	**Narrative (Section 3)**
Response to Literature	All-About Book	Personal Narrative
Book Review	How-to Piece	Memoir
Literary Essay	Informational Article	*Testimonio*
Persuasive Essay	Research or Lab Report	Oral History
Persuasive Letter	Informational Web Page	Biography
Advertisement	Oral Presentation	Narrative Fiction (realistic fiction, historical fiction, folktale, fantasy, fable, myth)
Blog	Documentary	
Documentary	Newsletter	

English Language Arts Standards: Writing ANCHOR 5

Writing Anchor 5: Develop and strengthen writing as needed by planning, revising, editing, rewriting, or trying a new approach.

Kindergarten	First	Second	Third	Fourth	Fifth
With guidance and support from adults, respond to questions and suggestions from peers and add details to strengthen writing as needed.	With guidance and support from adults, focus on a topic, respond to questions and suggestions from peers, and add details to strengthen writing as needed.	With guidance and support from adults and peers, focus on a topic and strengthen writing as needed by revising and editing.	With guidance and support from adults, develop and strengthen writing as needed by planning, revising, and editing. (Editing for conventions should demonstrate command of language standards 1–3 up to and including grade 3.)	With guidance and support from peers and adults, develop and strengthen writing as needed by planning, revising, and editing. (Editing for conventions should demonstrate command of language standards 1–3 up to and including grade 4.)	With guidance and support from peers and adults, develop and strengthen writing as needed by planning, revising, editing, rewriting, or trying a new approach. (Editing for conventions should demonstrate command of language standards 1–3 up to and including grade 5.)

Decision Tree for **Writing** ANCHOR 5

Is now a good time for focused instruction in relation to Writing Anchor 5?

Anchor 5 requires that students *develop and strengthen writing as needed by planning, revising, editing, rewriting, or trying a new approach.* The lessons and minilessons featured in Sections 1–4 are designed to support students as they work within the planning, drafting, and revising phases. Therefore, the emphasis in Section 5 is on *integrating* these processes with an added focus on *editing.* To support your students in developing skill in this area, you can implement three types of instruction:

| Demonstration
Page 136 | Collaborative Engagement
Page 147 | Independent Application
Page 151 |

It is recommended that you implement an overarching lesson first, followed by a formative assessment. The overarching lesson for Anchor 5 focuses on integrating the processes of planning, drafting, revising, and editing—with the instructional focus on editing. After analyzing the assessment data, you can use the information below to plan your subsequent instruction, considering whether to implement the lessons with the whole class or small groups.

Minilessons

When your students are ready to work with editing, consider the following:

- Quick Editing Minilessons (page 143)
- Using an Editing Checklist (page 143)
- Using Copy Editing Symbols (page 144)
- Encouraging the Circling of Suspicious Spellings (page 144)
- Studying Correct or Incorrect Usage (page 145)
- Using an Editing Circle (page 145)
- Playing with Punctuation (page 146)
- Opportunities for Rereading (page 146)

Collaborative Engagement

Collaboration in relation to Anchor 5 can be set up to support development of editing skills and of the conventions that support them. Consider the following:

- Analyzing and Evaluating Writing Samples from the Classroom (page 147)
- Analyzing and Evaluating Mentor Text (page 147)
- Conferring with the Teacher (page 148)
- Conferring with Peers (page 149)

Independent Application

Anchor 5 competencies are applied to the independent application experiences described in Sections 1–3. No new applications (text types/genres) are described for Anchor 5). After drafts are created (Sections 1–3) and fine-tuned and revised (Section 4), they can be edited using the processes described in Section 5.

Demonstration

Anchor 5 requires that students *develop and strengthen writing as needed by planning, revising, and editing.* The goal is that students will come to understand writing as a *process*, and that they will develop strategies for each phase that result in clear and coherent pieces appropriately crafted for the intended audience.

The lessons featured in Sections 1–4 are designed to support students as they work within the planning, drafting, and revising phases. Therefore, the emphasis in Section 5 is on *integrating* these processes, with an added focus on *editing*. Anchor 5 is the second of the standards within the *Production and Distribution of Writing* category, and as such, editing becomes a relevant component.

Success with Anchor 5 depends in great part on students understanding the concept of *process*. More than sitting down for one session, putting pencil to paper, and then being finished the very next moment, a natural part of writing is to play with a piece and tweak it to meet our specific goals. We *revise* when our ideas could use development, or when our language could be made more clear and concise. Ideas for teaching revision are addressed in Section 4. We *edit* when surface features such as capitalization, punctuation, and spelling could use work. Ideas for teaching editing are addressed in the present section. You will notice that the grade-level expectations for Anchor 5 indicate that written pieces should show command of Common Core Language standards 1–3, up to and including what is listed for the grade level. Figure 5–3 shows these expectations.

Overarching Lesson

To prepare for this lesson, be ready to take a piece of your own writing from planning through to editing. Keep the piece very short so you can show the entire process over the course of one or two days. Use a text type you have already taught (see Sections 1–3) so that you can place your focus on editing.

1. **Purpose.** Tell students that you are going to demonstrate working through a piece from planning to editing. *Note:* You may at some time find it helpful to work with students to collaboratively create a poster outlining all of the writing phases (see Figure 5–1).

2. **Expectations.** Briefly show students the expectations for Anchor 5 at your grade level (use information from Figures 5–2 and 5–3) and let them know that today you will be helping them work with editing. *Note:* Rather than extensively emphasizing any specific skill, the overarching lesson is used to set the general expectation for Anchor 5 and to identify areas in which students might benefit from more specific support with editing.

3. **Demonstration**

   - Show students how you take a piece through the phases of planning, drafting, and revising. Intentionally leave errors in capitalization, punctuation, and/or spelling.

   - Edit the piece, referring to the grade-level guidelines featured in Figure 5–3. Emphasize that your editing comes last, after you have your ideas written down and revised for meaning. Make it clear that a need for revision and editing does not mean a part of the process has failed; revision and editing are natural parts of the writing process.

4. **Student Writing.** Arrange adequate time for students to continue working on their current pieces, ensuring that each student attends appropriately to editing. Let students know that you will be evaluating their work to inform your next steps in instruction.

5. **Assessment.** Observe student processes and products to determine how well your class is meeting the expectations for Anchor 5. Using a class record (Figure 5–4) will offer an initial overview of what the class needs in terms of editing support, as well showing individual students' growth from a pre- to a postassessment.

Using Assessment to Inform Instruction

If the class record (Figure 5–4) shows that most students could use instruction in a particular area, it is advisable to keep the class together for the minilessons. If the record shows varied needs, then provide a mix of minilessons, pulling students in to work with you as needed. The decision tree on page 135 can help you to set your course.

Figure 5–1

Writing Is a Process

Planning

- Identify the topic.
- Identify the genre or format.
- Identify the purpose and audience.
- Think through the information that will be included. This may be done by drawing, talking, using a map, or jotting down notes.
- Ask, "Do I have sufficient knowledge about and interest in this topic?"

Drafting

- Write to get ideas down without worrying extensively about conventions.
- Focus on creating meaningful content. Use a checklist focused on grade-level expectations for structure.
- Keep in mind that drafts typically undergo revision and editing.
- **Language Standard 3** is emphasized in this phase.

Revising

- Rework for clarity and coherence.
- Rework for appropriateness to task, purpose, and audience.
- Share with peers and the teacher through planned conferences and small-group meetings. Rework based on comments.
- **Language Standard 1** is emphasized in this phase.

Editing

- Read the piece with conventions in mind, making needed changes.
- Work with guidance from the teacher and peers to look for errors.
- Use a checklist showing grade-level expectations for conventions.
- **Language Standard 2** is emphasized in this phase.

Publication

- Consider whether the piece should be taken to publication.
- Consider the most appropriate way to reach intended audience.
- Share the work with the audience.

Figure 5–2

CHECKLIST OF EXPECTATIONS FOR WRITING ANCHOR 5

Kindergarten

❏ Responds to questions and suggestions from peers.

❏ Adds details to strengthen writing.

Grade 1

❏ Focuses on a topic.

❏ Responds to questions and suggestions from peers.

❏ Adds details to strengthen writing.

Grade 2

❏ Focuses on a topic.

❏ Revises.

❏ Edits.

Grade 3

❏ Plans.

❏ Revises.

❏ Edits.

Grade 4

❏ Plans.

❏ Revises.

❏ Edits.

Grade 5

❏ Plans.

❏ Revises.

❏ Edits.

❏ Rewrites.

❏ Tries new approach as needed.

Note: Section 5 does not include a class record for documenting complete student competency in relation to Writing Anchor 5. It is recommended that observations about student participation in writing processes be conducted informally, using anecdotal notes as needed. The class records for Section 5 are focused on the conventions outlined in *Language Standard 2*. As specified in the Anchor 5 writing standards, student editing should show command of Language Standard 2 competencies up to and including grade level. Please note that elements the Language Standards 1 and 3 are addressed in various places throughout Sections 1–4. There you find with commentary and ideas set off in Language Standard boxes.

Figure 5–3

Editing for Conventions of Capitalization, Punctuation, and Spelling (Language Standard 2)

Kindergarten	First Grade	Second Grade
Capitals First word in sentence and "I"	**Capitals** Dates and names of people	**Capitals** Holidays, product names, geographic names
Punctuation Recognize and name end punctuation for sentences	**Punctuation** End punctuation for sentences Commas in date and to separate words in a series	**Punctuation** Commas for greetings and closings of letters Apostrophes for contractions and frequently occurring possessives
Spelling A letter or letters for most consonant and short-vowel sounds Phonetic spelling for simple words	**Spelling** Conventional for words with common patterns and for frequently occurring irregular words Phonetic spelling for untaught words	**Spelling** Spelling patterns are generalized Resources consulted as needed
Third Grade	**Fourth Grade**	**Fifth Grade**
Capitals Appropriate words in titles	**Capitals** Uses correct capitalization	**Capitals** Uses correct capitalization
Punctuation Commas in addresses Commas and quotation marks to set off dialogue Apostrophes for possessives	**Punctuation** Commas and quotation marks to mark direct speech and quotations from text Commas before coordinating conjunctions	**Punctuation** Punctuation to separate items in a series Comma to separate introductory element from the rest of the sentence Comma to set off words and questions, and to indicate direct address Underlining, quotation marks, or italics to indicate titles of works
Spelling Conventional for high-frequency words and other studied words and for adding suffixes to base words Spelling patterns generalized Resources consulted as needed	**Spelling** Grade-appropriate words correct with references consulted as needed	**Spelling** Grade-appropriate words correct with references consulted as needed

Figure 5–4

K–5 Class Record for Language Conventions (Language Standard 2)*

Grade Level: _____

Student Names	Grade-Level Expectations					
	Capitals		Punctuation		Spelling	
	Date	Date	Date	Date	Date	Date

0 = Not Present   **1 = Could Use Development**   **2 = Developed**

*See Figure 5–3 or Common Core Language Standard 2 for specific grade-level expectations.

ANCHOR

5

Minilessons

The minilessons in Section 5 are focused on editing. A central principle to keep in mind for editing instruction is that students do not become motivated to edit just so they can be "good" writers. Motivation for editing comes from a desire to meaningfully communicate. Therefore, we teach concepts and skills for editing within the context of authentic student writing, using pieces going to publication as well as our observations of students' patterns of error to guide our next steps in instruction.

Quick Editing Minilessons

Project a sentence, paragraph, or short text with a few errors of *one* type (capitalization, punctuation, spelling). You may use your own writing or a piece of student writing. Collaborate with students to repair the errors. Over time, include more than one error type, encouraging students to use a checklist as necessary (see the lesson on using editing checklists) to be sure they have considered all key expectations for your grade level. For students who master grade-level competencies, move up to the next level so that they continue to receive appropriate support. After students participate in editing minilessons, ask them to look for and correct the errors in their own writing. Hold group editing conferences to support students with similar editing needs.

Opportunity to Emphasize Language Standard 1

> In addition to leaving errors of capitalization, punctuation, and spelling, leave errors of grammar and usage (see Language Standard 1).

Using an Editing Checklist

This lesson is designed to help students understand the complete set of grade-level expectations for conventions that you will have for their published pieces. Figure 5–3 shows the expectations for English capitalization, punctuation, and spelling as described in Common Core Language Standard 2.

1. Choose one element or convention at a time from the list and show students how you review and edit your own writing or a piece of student writing in light of your chosen focus. Be sure the examples include convention requirements from both your grade level and previous grade levels.

2. Collaboratively (over time) develop a checklist that students can refer back to as they edit. Add one element at a time until the checklist is complete.

3. Regularly remind students that these are important concepts they should check with each piece they publish.

Using Copy Editing Symbols

Establish a set of copy editing symbols for the class to use (as in Figure 5–5). Having common symbols will help you understand your students' editing work, and will offer a way for peers to make suggestions without directly correcting the work of others. Demonstrate how to use the symbols with a piece of your own writing.

Encouraging the Circling of Suspicious Spellings

Show students how to read through their writing and circle words they think may be spelled incorrectly. They should write the "suspicious" words in three different ways to see if they can generate the correct spelling. Students may also bring the circled words to a teacher or peer conference, or use resources around the room to seek out conventional spellings. Resources may include word walls, familiar books, content-area trade books, textbooks, picture dictionaries, personal word banks, or another child. Be sure to demonstrate

Figure 5–5

Editing Symbols

∧ #	Add a space.	I learned toswim. ∧ #
∧	Add a word.	to I learned swim. ∧
/	Remove a word.	I learned tø to swim.
≡	Change to capital.	i learned to swim. ≡
/	Change to lower case.	I Ⱡearned to swim.
⊙ ? ⸴	Add a period, question mark, or comma.	I learned to swim⊙
SP ⬭	Check your spelling.	SP I (lerned) to swim.

the expectations and processes for using these resources. Conferences should involve looking for patterns of error (such as word endings, word parts, or high-frequency words). Personal word banks can be created to support conventional spelling of key words or parts.

Studying Correct or Incorrect Usage

Highlighting correct or incorrect usage (capitalization, punctuation, spelling, grammar) can be a useful practice for drawing student attention to conventions in writing and making the editing process concrete.

1. Using a piece of your own writing or student writing, show students how to use highlighters of different colors to mark certain conventions. They may mark correct or incorrect usage—or both. For example, using Figure 5–3 as a guide, you might direct students to highlight correctly used capitals with pink and missing or incorrectly used capitals with yellow.

2. After the conventions are highlighted, review them with students and collaboratively fix the errors with a pen or pencil.

3. After practicing with your guidance, students can use highlighters to go through and check their own writing or a peer's writing for correct or incorrect usage. This work may be brought to a peer or teacher conference for discussion. Focus on helping students identify their patterns of error, such as often omitting beginning capitals or not using the possessive apostrophe.

Using an Editing Circle

Editing circles are teams of students that meet to provide editing support for an entire group. To prepare for the lesson, select a group of three to five students to work with you in a "fishbowl" that allows the other students to observe. Select a teacher or student writing sample containing errors of convention.

1. Have participating students sit in a circle around a document projector or SMART Board as the class looks on. Give each student a different color of pencil.

2. Guide each student to edit the piece with a focus on a different convention. For example, one student would focus on capitals, another on punctuation, and another on spelling. Refer to the students as the "capitals editor," the "spelling editor," and so on.

> **Opportunity to Emphasize**
> **Language Standard 1**
>
> ❯ Use pieces with errors of grammar and usage, such as with irregular nouns or reflexive pronouns, so that students may learn strategies for improving them.

3. After the demonstration of what each editor should do, show the students how the process will work when every member brings a piece for peer editing. The students will sit in a circle just as they are now and pass their papers to the left. Each student will use one colored pencil and act as editor in the role he or she had in step 2, and then pass the paper around the circle. Groups may use a timer, and be instructed to spend just one or two minutes working with each piece. After the pieces make it back to their respective authors, students read through the edits and ask questions of the other editors as needed.

Playing with Punctuation

Students are so accustomed to seeing punctuation in published text that sometimes it takes actually removing it to show its impact. Remove the punctuation from a short piece of writing. (Choose a text that includes the punctuation concepts your students need to develop.) Have partners or teams add appropriate punctuation, and then compare their results with other teams before looking at the original piece.

Opportunities for Rereading

Errors in convention often become apparent when students come back to a piece after putting it down for a while (even for a day), or when they read their work aloud to a peer. Regularly offer rereading opportunities during writing time, or at the beginning or end of writing periods. Allow students to use a highlighter to mark areas to be fixed, or be sure they have pencils with good erasers.

Collaborative Engagement

To support development of the key concepts for Anchor 5, particularly as they relate to editing, arrange for students to engage in collaborative analysis and evaluation experiences, peer conferences, and teacher conferences.

Analyzing and Evaluating Writing Samples from the Classroom

After students have worked with you to develop understandings about processes and expectations for editing, give individuals a sample of student writing (or use teacher writing if you don't yet have a student sample) and ask them to analyze it in light of particular criteria. They should refer to your grade-level checklist (as in Figure 5–3). You may or may not use text containing errors of convention. Allow students to mark up the text so they have a reference point for their discussions. When working with Anchor 5, select from questions such as those featured in Figure 5–6. After the individual evaluations, groups or partners meet to compare findings.

Analyzing and Evaluating Mentor Text

Professionally published texts that students have particularly enjoyed offer a useful tool for investigating the conventions necessary for effective communication. The *familiarity* of the text will provide a context for understanding

> **Opportunity to Emphasize Language Standard 1**
>
> › Discuss the characteristics of a sentence.
>
> › Guide students to analyze sentences for grammar and usage, as appropriate.

ANCHOR 5

Figure 5–6

Questions for Evaluating Writing Samples in Relation to Anchor 5

- Where are capitals used? Are any capitals missing?
- How is end punctuation used? Is it used correctly? Is any end punctuation missing?
- Do we notice any spellings to fix? How could we fix them?
- Are any commas used? Why are they used? Are they used correctly? Are any commas missing?
- Are any apostrophes used? Why are they used? Are they used correctly? Are any apostrophes missing?
- How is dialogue punctuated? Is it punctuated correctly?

Figure 5–7

Questions for Evaluating Mentor Text in Relation to Anchor 5

- Which words are capitalized? Is there a pattern?
- What end punctuation does the author use? Why did the author make this choice?
- How does the author use commas?
- What are the different ways apostrophes are used? Is there a pattern?
- How does the author use punctuation to show dialogue?
- How does the author use punctuation to help show mood or tone?
- How does the author use punctuation to show what the character is thinking or feeling?

the use of conventions, and the *appreciation* for the piece will help create motivation for studying the author's usage.

1. After your students read, view, or listen to a text, set them up in groups and give each group a copy of the text, directing them to a specific section as appropriate. Assign the groups to work through one to three guiding questions, such as those featured in Figure 5–7. You can differentiate by having different groups work with different questions or texts.

2. If several groups are working on this project, arrange time for the groups to report and compare their findings and observations.

Conferring with the Teacher

Conferences are an excellent forum for discussing and supporting editing processes. As a rule of thumb, keep the focus on *teaching the writer* rather than *perfecting the piece*. Rather than pointing out every error, help the student identify lasting errors or patterns of error. Rather than finding errors *for* the student, show the student how to edit for key types. It can be tempting to help the student create a flawless piece, but it is generally more effective to focus on one key concept or strategy that the student can carefully consider and internalize.

When conferring in relation to Anchor 5, keep your focus on Anchor 5 objectives. Organizing the conference with a predictable set of prompts and questions can help students know what to expect and be ready to show you their thinking. See Figure 5–8.

Figure 5–8

Conference Routine

- **Open the conversation.** *How are things going in terms of editing (refer to capitalization, punctuation, grammar, and/or spelling)? Will you read this to me?*

- **Identify notable strengths.** *I see that you are (capitalizing/using this type of punctuation, spelling commonly used words correctly).*

- **Identify one teaching point.** *What do you think you should focus on editing? Can you show me how you will start? Or I have one thing I want you to work on and I'm going to help you get started.*

- **Send the student away with something manageable to develop.** *Let's get you started on this and then next time we meet we can talk about how it's going.*

Conferring with Peers

Children can be very capable and responsible responders to their peers' writing, especially when they are given some starting expectations for their conversations. After they have some experience working through the editing process, coach them to work in peer conferences or small groups through any of the processes featured in Figure 5–9. You may wish to occasionally allow students to invite a peer to an editing conference to help them prepare for collaborative revision.

FOR ENGLISH LEARNERS

Correcting an entire piece so that it reads perfectly in English can provide helpful exposure to conventions, but equally as powerful is sitting together with the student to work on a specific competency such as identifying a key spelling pattern or using acceptable syntax. Effective instruction involves both exposure to and instruction in conventions.

Figure 5–9

Peer Conference Plans

Listen to the author read the text aloud. Afterward, together with the author, ask:

- Are capitals in place?
- Is end punctuation in place?
- Are commas in place?
- Are apostrophes used correctly?
- Is the title punctuated correctly?
- Do we notice any incorrect spellings? If so, how could we correct them?
- What other areas could use a fix?

Independent Application

For independent application, students are expected to apply the concepts taught through editing minilessons to the types of writing emphasized in Sections 1–3, as shown in Figure 5–10.

Figure 5–10

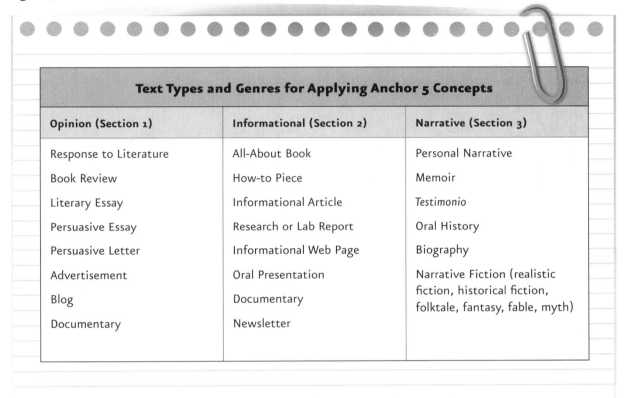

Text Types and Genres for Applying Anchor 5 Concepts		
Opinion (Section 1)	**Informational (Section 2)**	**Narrative (Section 3)**
Response to Literature	All-About Book	Personal Narrative
Book Review	How-to Piece	Memoir
Literary Essay	Informational Article	*Testimonio*
Persuasive Essay	Research or Lab Report	Oral History
Persuasive Letter	Informational Web Page	Biography
Advertisement	Oral Presentation	Narrative Fiction (realistic fiction, historical fiction, folktale, fantasy, fable, myth)
Blog	Documentary	
Documentary	Newsletter	

PRODUCTION AND DISTRIBUTION OF WRITING

ANCHOR 6

English Language Arts Standards: Writing ANCHOR 6

Writing Anchor 6: Use technology, including the Internet, to produce and publish writing and to interact and collaborate with others.

Kindergarten	First	Second	Third	Fourth	Fifth
With guidance and support from adults, explore a variety of digital tools to produce and publish writing, including in collaboration with peers.	With guidance and support from adults, use a variety of digital tools to produce and publish writing, including in collaboration with peers.	With guidance and support from adults, use a variety of digital tools to produce and publish writing, including in collaboration with peers.	With guidance and support from adults, use technology to produce and publish writing (using keyboarding skills) as well as to interact and collaborate with others.	With some guidance and support from adults, use technology, including the Internet, to produce and publish writing as well as to interact and collaborate with others; demonstrate sufficient command of keyboarding skills to type a minimum of one page in a single sitting.	With some guidance and support from adults, use technology, including the Internet, to produce and publish writing as well as to interact and collaborate with others; demonstrate sufficient command of keyboarding skills to type a minimum of two pages in a single sitting.

The technology practices are taught in conjunction with the independent applications described in Sections 1–3.

Note: Keyboarding skills are not addressed in this book.

Demonstration

Technological advances in the twenty-first century have stretched writers of all ages. Even the youngest students have moved beyond using paper and pencil to using a combination of modalities including print, images, sound, and video. With new technologies come new genres such as blogs and web pages, and new formatting challenges involving hyperlinks, menu bars, and image placement. And with the Internet at our fingertips, we are now collaborating and communicating more broadly than ever before. It is not surprising that the Common Core State Standards call for students to develop skill in using technology *to produce and publish writing* and *to interact and collaborate with others* (Anchor 6). Having capability with technology is a part of twenty-first-century literacy.

It follows that teaching toward technological literacy is a part of twenty-first-century teaching. An important role for today's teacher is to help students develop knowledge and skills for designing and formatting text in the digital environment; for integrating text with images, sound, and video; and for selecting the media and outlets that are most appropriate to task, purpose, and audience.

The grade-level expectations for Anchor 6 leave open a range of possibilities for exploring these concepts. Rather than defining specific uses of technology for each grade level, students across the K–5 range are simply expected to use digital tools and resources to *produce, publish, interact,* and *collaborate*. The specifics may vary and will in large part depend on the equipment and the Internet access you have in your classroom and school. Therefore, in Section 6 you will find a set of versatile ideas for making use of technology within the writing curriculum. The ideas can be adapted for settings in which not much technology is yet available, and for settings in which technology use is already widespread. All of the technology options are applied in conjunction with the independent applications described in Sections 1–3.

Structuring the Lessons

Various options are available for demonstrating the uses of technology in producing, publishing, interacting, and collaborating around writing. It is recommended that you connect all demonstrations to the writing your students are currently doing so they can use technology to support and enhance their work. Consider the following scheduling options.

Whole Class

If you have access to a computer lab or to mobile equipment for each student, it makes good sense to provide demonstrations that allow for simultaneous hands-on exploration by all. Show students the procedures step by step, allowing them to try the processes on their individual devices.

Small Group

Regardless of whether you have access to devices for every student in the class, there are times when small-group lessons are more appropriate than whole-class lessons. For example, if students are learning to use a complicated program or if you know they will be unsure of how to merge content and technology, you may want to work with one group at a time to provide individualized support.

Small groups are also a good time for students to become instructors. If you have students with expertise, or if you can train a small group to work with other students, the "experts" can walk the other members of the class through the procedures for using the technology. This may occur in stations or at a computer lab.

Guidelines for Using Technology to Support the Writing Curriculum

- Select technology that clearly supports student development of central aspects of the writing process (planning, drafting, revising, editing, and/or publishing). Avoid uses that reflect activity unrelated to the curriculum (such as random games and videos).

- Demonstrate how to use tools and applications before assigning students to try them on their own. After the initial demonstration, allow time for open exploration. Playing around with the options will help students better understand how to use them creatively and in purposeful ways.

- Set your technology demonstrations within the context of your writing demonstrations. For example, if you want students to learn to import images into a Word document, use a real piece of your writing to show how the images serve to enrich or extend the text. We want students to use technology to improve and develop pieces rather than just for the sake of knowing how to use it.

- Teach one tool or application at a time. For example, instead of teaching all the affordances of a word-processing program at once, show the revision tools on one day, the spell check on another day, the thesaurus on another, and so on.

- Use technology that is versatile and can be used in a variety of contexts. You will spend valuable time teaching how to use tools and processes, so choose applications that can be used for multiple purposes, by many students, over the course of the year.

- When selecting technology, be wary of applications that may limit your students' participation in the writing process. For example, consider whether the tool allows adequate space for text and whether it allows for saving and returning to the document for revising and editing.

- Monitor computer activity to ensure that your students do not spend exorbitant amounts of time playing with features such as Word art, fonts, and images at the expense of actual composing, revising, and editing. You may need to set a time limit for working with such features, or set up special sessions for incorporating them.

- Teach effective discourses and etiquette for collaborating online. Show students exactly what is expected in terms of collaboration. Without the luxury of talk, facial expressions, gestures, and backing up to clarify, we have to be extra vigilant in the digital environment to ensure our written words communicate what we intend and do not offend others.

- Teach students to use technology safely and responsibly, reviewing with them any district guidelines for students. Always be aware of whether the tools you are using are set for general access or school-only access. There should be policies in place to help you determine whether certain uses are permitted.

- Technology is always changing, so be sure to stay abreast of new developments. *Education Week* offers a steady stream of articles that can be accessed for free: www.edweek.org/ew/section/free-content/index.html.

Producing and Publishing Writing

Technology can support and enhance writing in all phases of the process from planning to publication. As a rule of thumb, select for quality rather than quantity. A few sound, well-understood uses will be more effective than a stream of tools that might be partially used and/or understood.

Word Processors

Even with the scores of technology applications available for use in K–5 classrooms, word-processing programs are still one of the most valuable for producing and publishing writing. Word processors offer mapping and planning tools; a variety of possible formats for publishing; ease of revision; applications that support editing (such as spell and grammar checks); the potential for links to electronic material; and storage and sharing capability. They also offer the potential for more fluent writing than some children can muster without a keyboard (Graham 2008). OpenOffice (http://download .openoffice.fm/free/) and Microsoft Word (www.microsoftstore.com/store/ msstore/en_US/pd/productID.216673600) are recommended. OpenOffice may be downloaded for free.

Publishers

Publishing programs offer built-in formatting that is typically not available through a word processor. Publishing programs are particularly useful for formatting newsletters, brochures, booklets, and flyers (see Anchors 1–3). The following programs, which offer varied levels of sophistication, are recommended for use in the elementary classroom.

- **Canvastic** (www.canvastic.net/): free

- **Printing Press** (www.readwritethink.org/classroom-resources/ student-interactives/readwritethink-printing-press-30036.html): free

- **Microsoft Publisher** (http://office.microsoft.com/en-us/publisher/): fee for product

- **PagePlus** (www.serif.com/desktop-publishing-software/): free

Web-Based Composing Tools

Web-based composing tools offer young writers a variety that extends beyond typical word-processing or publishing program features. Along with providing a designated space for text and images, web-based tools often provide scaffolds for what to include (such as prompts to add titles, images, drawings, or sound; guidance to include key structural elements such as characters, setting, problem, and resolution for a story; or guidance to include an opening statement, reasons, and a conclusion for an opinion piece). One caution is to check ahead to see that there is enough space for your students to write with depth. Another is to determine whether the material can be saved and developed at a later time. Following are some web-based tools that can be used to support student writing in relation to Anchors 1–3.

Tool	Link	Description	Use
Persuasion Map	www.readwritethink.org/classroom-resources/student-interactives/persuasion-30034.html	ReadWriteThink's persuasion map guides students to lay out the key components of an argument/opinion as specified for Anchor 1. Student work may be saved, emailed, or printed.	*Use with Anchor 1.*
Letter Generator	www.readwritethink.org/classroom-resources/student-interactives/letter-generator-30005.html	ReadWriteThink's letter generator guides students to write a friendly letter or a business letter that includes all the important parts. Students working with Anchor 1 (argument/opinion writing) can use the platform to write an entire letter and then print, save, or email the final product.	*Use with Anchor 1.*
Card Making Tool	www.kerpoof.com	Kerpoof offers a card-making tool that includes space for text and images. Students in the early phases of learning to write opinion pieces (Anchor 1) can use this tool to express an *opinion with reasons*. For example, "You are the best dad in the world because. . . ." "You are my favorite author *because*. . . ." Cards can be saved, printed, or emailed.	*Use with Anchor 1.*
Poster Making Tool	http://edu.glogster.com/what-is-glogster-edu/	Glogster's multimedia poster tool allows students to make posters that include text, images, audio, video, sound, and data. Students can use this tool to individually or collaboratively develop pieces such as book reviews, advertisements, or informational presentations. Posters can be saved and shared as a presentation or made available through a link to a wiki, blog, or website.	*Use with Anchors 1 and 2.*
Essay Tool	www.readwritethink.org/classroom-resources/student-interactives/essay-30063.html	ReadWriteThink's essay tool guides students to outline the key components of an essay on any topic. Students may write a persuasive essay (Anchor 1), an informational piece (Anchor 2), or a personal narrative (Anchor 3). The product can be saved, emailed, or printed.	*Use with Anchors 1, 2, and 3.*

(continues)

Tool	Link	Description	Use
Templates for Multiple Genres	http://teacher.scholastic.com/writewit/index.htm	Scholastic's *Writing with Writers* site offers guidelines and templates for writing in various genres, including biographies, folktales, mysteries, myths, news articles, and book reviews. Students using the site are prompted to include the key components within the genres to generate a complete piece. For example, students writing biographies are prompted to pick an important person, brainstorm key questions to answer, and list key facts about the person. Students writing book reviews are prompted to describe the setting and the main characters, and to offer a glimpse of the plot without giving it away. The site contains examples of student writing in each genre, and a platform for students to publish their own work through the site.	*Use with Anchors 1, 2, and 3.*
Storybird	www.storybird.com	Storybird contains art images that students use as a basis for creating text. Tags on the art allow for searching in relation to topics. For example, students writing narrative fiction (Anchor 3) could search for character images of fairies, pirates, unicorns, or mythical creatures. Students writing informational text (Anchor 2) will find images that represent all kinds of nonfiction topics, such as apples, spring, boats, and the body. Students can choose one piece of art and write text or dialogue for it, or they can write a more extended book embedded with art images that can be saved and printed.	*Use with Anchors 1, 2, and 3.*
Story Tool	www.kerpoof.com	Kerpoof's *Tell a Story* tool provides a platform for students to write narratives (Anchor 3) that can be saved and shared electronically. The tool includes images that can be dragged to create settings and characters, speech bubbles for text, and a drawing tool.	*Use with Anchor 3.*
Story Map	www.readwritethink.org/files/resources/interactives/storymap/index.html	ReadWriteThink's story map site contains four tools that students can use to develop a character, a setting, a problem, or a resolution. The material can be printed and used as a resource in moving the piece from draft to finished product.	*Use with Anchor 3.*

Apps for Composing

As with the web-based tools described previously, many downloadable applications for iPads, iTouches, and other wireless devices can be used to support students in producing and publishing writing. Following are some versatile apps for use with K–5 students. It is recommended that you start with just one. Demonstrate how to use the app to create a piece of your own and then allow time and support for students to explore it. When your students are comfortable using one app, introduce another that offers new and different capabilities so they can eventually learn to choose from a set based on their task, purpose, and audience.

Tool	Link	Description	Use
Story Buddy 2	http://itunes.apple.com/us/app/storybuddy-2/id505856601?mt=8	*Story Buddy 2* allows students to create multipage texts that include print, photographs, drawings, and an audio recording. Students may use this app to compose narrative or informational pieces. Final products can be printed or shared by email.	*Use with Anchors 1, 2, and 3.*
Story Kit	http://itunes.apple.com/us/app/storykit/id329374595?mt=8	*Story Kit* allows students to create narrative or informational pieces that include text, drawings or photos, and sound. Finished products can be emailed and shared.	*Use with Anchors 1, 2, and 3.*
Popplet	http://popplet.com/	*Popplet* is an app designed for mapping and organizing ideas. Students create boxes (*popplets*) and add text, drawings, or photos (or a combination of these). Popplets can be organized and linked in a number of ways and used for planning a piece of writing, composing a complete descriptive piece in the form of a photo montage with captions, or composing a sequenced narrative with brief text.	*Use with Anchors 1, 2, and 3.*
Story Builder	http://itunes.apple.com/us/app/storybuilder/id402652939?mt=8	Students using *Story Builder* are prompted, step-by-step, to develop an audio narrative based on pictures with ready-made images. Student narratives can be saved and emailed.	*Use with Anchor 3.*
Story Patch	http://itunes.apple.com/us/app/story-patch/id388613157?mt=8	*Story Patch* allows students to create, edit, and share stories using ready-made images with photo backdrops.	*Use with Anchor 3.*

Digitally Created Visuals

Digitally created visuals can be used to enrich, extend, and economize the content students produce through writing. They may be used whether students are composing with paper and pencil, a word processor, or a digital tool that allows for upload. Consider the following:

Tool	Link	Description	Use
Webs, charts, diagrams		Students use the *Smart Art* feature from Microsoft Word or a similar program to create webs, charts, and diagrams.	*Use with Anchors 1 and 2.*
Graphs	http://nces.ed.gov/ nceskids/createagraph/ default.aspx	Students using this tool can create a bar, a line, an area, a pie, or an XY graph. Graphs created using this site may be labeled, saved, and printed.	*Use with Anchors 1 and 2.*
Maps	https:// maps.google.com/	Google provides satellite and road map images of virtually any location around the world. Students can use the maps to identify locations in relation to a project or to create *mash-ups* (a combination of two or more types of media) that extend the information provided by the map. For example, they might add to a state map captioned images of important figures who were born in various towns; descriptions of the natural resources prevalent in various regions; or links to information related to the state.	*Use with Anchors 1, 2, and 3.*
Clip art		Students use the clip art feature from a word-processing program to import images into a document, or they print the images and merge them into a paper-and-pencil creation.	*Use with Anchors 1, 2, and 3.*
Photographs and videos		Students use digital equipment to photograph or videotape images needed for a current piece, and import them into a word-processed or web-based document, or they can print photographs and add them to a paper-and-pencil document. Students may also use photographs downloaded from the web or from a collection prepared by the teacher.	*Use with Anchors 1, 2, and 3.*
Word clouds	www.abcya.com/ word_clouds.htm or www.wordle.net	Students type or paste text into a box to generate a "word cloud" that contains an arrangement of the most frequently used words in the text. Word clouds illuminate key vocabulary and concepts in a piece, and offer the reader a way to consider the concepts through a new lens.	*Use with Anchors 1 and 2.*

Interacting and Collaborating with Others

Along with using technology to produce and publish writing, the Common Core State Standards call for students to use technology to interact and collaborate with others. Several possibilities follow.

Document Projectors

Document projectors are a useful tool for collaborating within the writing classroom. In their simplest form, they project a hard copy image of a document for the whole class to view. Most projectors offer zoom features, and some offer video or image capture for saving on a computer. Students and teachers can use a document projector to show their work to the class (which is especially important when detailed illustrations and images are used), to highlight varying aspects of craft and convention, and to demonstrate or collaborate on processes of revision and editing.

Interactive Whiteboards

Interactive whiteboards allow students and teachers to collaboratively create and explore multimedia content. They can be used for brainstorming topics, for projecting pieces of writing to revise and edit, for multimedia student presentations, and for teacher demonstrations of writing processes or computer skills, online research processes, and how to use interactive websites. Students can email pieces of writing to you, which can then be used for demonstration purposes. Most interactive whiteboards can save and store information for later use.

Web-Based Document Sharing Platforms

Document sharing platforms allow students to create, store, and simultaneously work on documents and presentations and to save the material for later revision or editing. Multiple users can work on the same project at the same time. Students can use document sharing platforms for activities such as brainstorming, collaboratively collecting information (such as on a timeline or web), collaborative writing, or collaborative revision and editing. Some platforms allow for shared documents to be set up as websites that include pictures, links, and video and can be used for multimedia presentations. The following platforms are recommended:

- **Google Docs** (www.docs.google.com)
- **Titanpad** (www.titanpad.com)
- **Wikispaces** (www.wikispaces.com)

Student-Created Websites and Web Pages

Websites and web pages can be created for use solely within the classroom—or to share with families, other students in the school, or beyond. (Check your school policies.) If you do not have access through your school to a tool for creating a website, consider weebly.com or wallwisher.com. Weebly offers various formats for publishing pages as well as a blogging platform. Wallwisher allows contributors to compose and post a short message on an electronic sticky note. Both platforms allow for linking to videos or other websites.

Blogs

A blog is a public forum that students can use to express viewpoints and share expertise with classmates, schoolmates, or beyond. For example, students might set up a blog to discuss a current issue the class is exploring or to share experiences in relation to a particular topic. If your school doesn't have a system in place, try Edublogs (http://edublogs.org). This website offers a free platform set up for educational purposes and includes easy-to-follow guidelines for implementing the entire process. Your blogs can be set for complete privacy (such as allowing only the teacher to log in, or only the teacher and students, or only the teacher and other teachers in the school). Before getting started, check with your administrative office to learn about any existing tools or policies your school may have to guide the process.

Social Media and Networking Sites

Social media and networking sites such as Facebook or Twitter can be used for a variety of purposes related to the writing process. It is recommended that you set pages up for private viewing (classroom only, or families may be included). Social networking sites may be used in the following ways:

- To publish (post) student-written news from the classroom.
- To collect and share links on key topics being studied.
- To post short pieces of writing to which other students may respond.
- To post questions or prompts to which students respond.

Independent Application

For independent application, students are expected to use technology to develop and produce the types of writing emphasized in Sections 1–3, as shown in Figure 6–1.

Figure 6–1

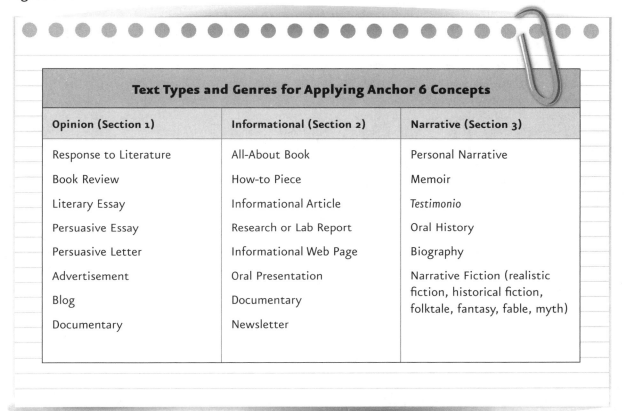

Text Types and Genres for Applying Anchor 6 Concepts		
Opinion (Section 1)	**Informational (Section 2)**	**Narrative (Section 3)**
Response to Literature	All-About Book	Personal Narrative
Book Review	How-to Piece	Memoir
Literary Essay	Informational Article	*Testimonio*
Persuasive Essay	Research or Lab Report	Oral History
Persuasive Letter	Informational Web Page	Biography
Advertisement	Oral Presentation	Narrative Fiction (realistic fiction, historical fiction, folktale, fantasy, fable, myth)
Blog	Documentary	
Documentary	Newsletter	

RESEARCH TO BUILD AND PRESENT KNOWLEDGE

ANCHOR 7

English Language Arts Standards: **Writing ANCHOR 7**

Writing Anchor 7: Conduct short as well as more sustained research projects based on focused questions, demonstrating understanding of the subject under investigation.

Kindergarten	First	Second	Third	Fourth	Fifth
Participate in shared research and writing projects (e.g., explore a number of books by a favorite author and express opinions about them).	Participate in shared research and writing projects (e.g., explore a number of "how-to" books on a given topic and use them to write a sequence of instructions).	Participate in shared research and writing projects (e.g., read a number of books on a single topic to produce a report; record science observations).	Conduct short research projects that build knowledge about a topic.	Conduct short research projects that build knowledge through investigation of different aspects of a topic.	Conduct short research projects that use several sources to build knowledge through investigation of different aspects of a topic.

Planning and Demonstration

Anchor 7 requires that students *engage in short research projects, demonstrating understanding of the subject under investigation.* The goal is that students will build knowledge about the topic, and at the same time learn processes of conducting and reporting research within the subject area at hand.

Within the elementary classroom, we can think of students conducting research in two central ways. One way is to gather and investigate information from print and digital sources. Students search and read with a particular research question in mind and organize and interpret the information in light of this question. Examples of questions students might ask when conducting print-based research are "What is the difference between a butterfly and a moth?" "What does a plant need to grow?" "How is ice cream made?" "Could humans ever live on Mars?" "Why are there Indian reservations in the United States?" The answers to the questions in print-based research are found in the texts students read.

Another way to conduct research is through actual scientific observation. As with print-based research, students seek information in relation to a particular question, but with observation, they find the answers by observing actual phenomena. Examples of questions students might ask when conducting observation-based research are "Do the ants in our farm prefer raisins, carrots, cheese, or cereal?" "Which conditions are best for plant growth?" "Which of Eric Carle's books are favored by most members of our class?" "What do local elders remember about our city?" The answers to the questions in observation-based research are found through planned experiences or experiments and are contextualized and given depth through the reading students do.

With Anchor 7 comes the important reminder that *knowledge related to conducting research* is a part of literacy. Readers and writers use certain skills and strategies that are unique to research, and we want kids to develop skill in this area so they can think and act knowledgeably as they engage in research-based experiences. Section 7 contains a suggested set of practices for supporting student research in your classroom.

Planning Research Opportunities

Few educators would disagree with the notion that students benefit from engaging in print- and observation-based research. Yet many of us feel that we could do more to bring research into the classroom. With this in mind, consider the following:

- If you have a curriculum for teaching social studies and science, it likely contains ideas for student research. Take a good look at the ideas provided, and determine which might make sense to develop in your setting—and when. It's not necessary to know all of the details ahead of time. The details will emerge when students begin to express their questions and interests—but think through the general areas that lend themselves to research, and lay out a timeline that includes the general topic and the probable type of research (print-based or observation-based) that students could use to explore it.

- If your teaching materials do not suggest specific ideas for research, look for your own opportunities in relation to the topics being studied. In what areas might students benefit from being guided to develop questions on a topic and to then engage in print- or observation-based research to answer them? Science and social studies lend themselves well to finding research opportunities, with knowledge of math being used within each of these areas, but you may also create opportunities through art, health, physical, or music education. Spreading into these areas often leads to rich opportunities for collaboration with the content teachers, and is a good way to spread the responsibility for teaching writing and research.

- As you are planning, it is a good idea to work within and across grade levels to ensure a comprehensive experience that progressively builds skill and sophistication. To get organized, it may help to lay out a plan showing what each grade level is doing. Figure 7–1 shows an example that can be adapted for use in your setting. The plan shows students at each grade level conducting six research projects per year.

Research can be as small as partnering up with another student to answer a question through reading—or as big as laying out a project that includes a key research question, a designated set of methods and materials, a

Figure 7–1

K–5 Research Plan						
	K	**1**	**2**	**3**	**4**	**5**
Print-Based Research	Science Social Studies Art	Science Social Studies Music	Science Social Studies Art	Science Social Studies Music	Science Social Studies Art	Science Social Studies Music
Interview	Social Studies (Interview classmate)	Social Studies (Interview family member)	Social Studies (Interview extended family member)		Social Studies (Interview community member)	
Survey	Language Arts	Social Studies		Language Arts		Social Studies
Observation	Science	Science	Science	Science	Science	Science
Experiment			Science	Science	Science	Science

set of findings, and a formal report. Go for variety and experiences that lend insight into content-area studies. Multiple experiences with research must be integrated across the curriculum and throughout the years if we hope for students to emerge as knowledgeable thinkers who can meet the challenges of the research standards and learn from and make an impact on others through their efforts.

Overarching Lesson

Just as demonstration supports all other aspects of writing, it supports students in learning the processes of conducting and writing about research. While specifics will vary across grade levels, content areas, and topics, the following procedures are universal and can be demonstrated as you launch each new project. You may wish to implement the lesson over several days so that students can work alongside you on their own projects and try out the practices as you go.

1. **State the project parameters.**

   - Tell students that they will be engaging in a research project, and that you will be demonstrating some of the key processes they will use.

   - State the overarching *topic parameters*, letting students know that they will be taking varied paths within. For example, while you might require that everyone focus on *our state* or *our families* or *what we eat for breakfast* or *the insect world* or *the birds at our feeder* or *owl pellets*, students can work individually or in groups to determine the specific questions they will pursue. *Note*: When students or groups take different paths and choose their own questions—real questions that they really want to know the answers to—enthusiasm runs high and the class can build a more broad body of knowledge than when the teacher dictates a singular path.

   - State the **collaboration parameters**, letting students know whether they will work individually or in groups. (You may allow them to form groups based on topics.)

   - State the **research parameters**, identifying whether you are planning for print- and/or observation-based research. Require that students stay within the research type you have selected. Briefly explain what the research will look like.

   - State the *presenting* or **publishing parameters**. For any given project, it is recommended that you choose one appropriate format for the class to use (such as a formal lab report or a page for an all-about book) so that you can integrate instruction related to structure (Anchors 1 to 3) with instruction related to content. Of particular use for presenting findings from research are the formats featured in Figure 7–2. These are described in Sections 1–3.

Figure 7–2

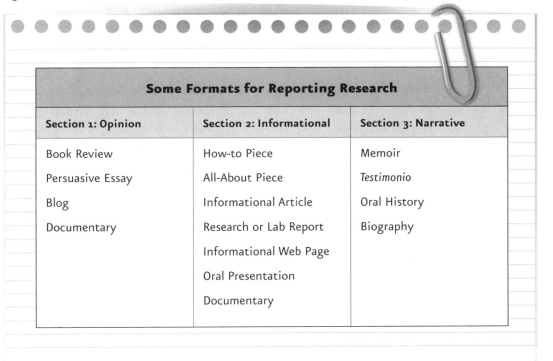

Some Formats for Reporting Research

Section 1: Opinion	Section 2: Informational	Section 3: Narrative
Book Review	How-to Piece	Memoir
Persuasive Essay	All-About Piece	*Testimonio*
Blog	Informational Article	Oral History
Documentary	Research or Lab Report	Biography
	Informational Web Page	
	Oral Presentation	
	Documentary	

2. **Identify your research question.**

- Show students your questioning processes in relation to the topic at hand, homing in on *one* question to use for demonstration. For example:

  - What does a house spider eat?

  - How is a spider web made? What is it for?

  - What happens when a fly lands on food?

  - Which type of gum can produce the biggest bubble?

  - What do our families do together after school?

  - What are the typical breakfast foods our families eat?

  - What do children do to be safe in their homes?

  - What do the members of our class think about the proposal to raise taxes to support the art institute?

- Guide students to start thinking about their own questions. *Note*: The best questions don't necessarily emerge at the beginning of a unit of study but instead may surface after students have had some time for hands-on investigation and/or reading in relation to the topic. As you move through the early phases of a unit of study, provide students with a research notebook and have them set aside a space for recording questions. You can demonstrate this process with your own notebook.

3. **Demonstrate the procedures for answering the question.** Show students how to systematically document information in relation to the research question you are using for demonstration. (Your question should directly reflect the type your students will be asking and answering.) Figures 8–1 and 8–2 in Section 8 provide forms for documenting, which may help your students stay focused. (Section 8 deals with using sources and gathering information in more depth.) Keep in mind that even the youngest students can collect information from books before they can read the text. (For example: What do bats eat? What do families do together? What does a moth's life cycle look like?)

4. **Discuss the medium for presenting findings.** Review the content and structural expectations for the written project, using your own project as an example. Demonstrate what you expect the students to do. As with any written piece, research-related pieces going to publication may be revised and edited as described in Sections 4 and 5. As your students move into their projects, bring in varied writing and research minilessons as needed (see Sections 1–6 and 8–9).

Collaborative and Independent Application

It is recommended that your research initiatives include plans for offering extensive guidance along the way. The following procedures for getting students started with projects and supporting them in working through each new project may be adapted according to your students' progress and needs across the school year:

1. Allow time for an initial exploration in relation to the topic at hand. Students may browse print and digital sources and/or engage in observation and hands-on exploration.

2. Work with the class to list possible research questions in relation to the topic, and then take one of three paths:

    - **Path 1:** Collaboratively choose one question and plan to work as a class to answer it, letting students take responsibility for parts of the process.

    - **Path 2:** Narrow the set of questions to no more than five. Form groups based on student choices. More than one group can pursue the same general question, refining the specifics, if appropriate, as the work carries them forward.

    - **Path 3:** Encourage each student to choose a question (or develop a related question) and plan to work independently or as the "principal investigator" to answer it.

3. Regardless of the path taken in step 2, choose a question to use for demonstration, and brainstorm how you might go about answering it. Brainstorm how to find answers to the remaining student—or group—questions as appropriate.

4. Support the students or groups in selecting and gathering texts or setting up materials to find answers to their questions. To support focused reading and observation, refer to techniques described in Sections 8 and 9.

5. Support students in writing up or presenting their findings. Refer to the independent applications in Figure 7–2 (from Sections 1–3) as you consider formats for presentation.

English Language Arts Standards: Writing ANCHOR 8

Writing Anchor 8: Gather relevant information from multiple print and digital sources, assess the credibility and accuracy of each source, and integrate the information while avoiding plagiarism.

Kindergarten	First	Second	Third	Fourth	Fifth
With guidance and support from adults, recall information from experiences or gather information from provided sources to answer a question.	With guidance and support from adults, recall information from experiences or gather information from provided sources to answer a question.	Recall information from experiences or gather information from provided sources to answer a question.	Recall information from experiences or gather information from print and digital sources; take brief notes on sources and sort evidence into provided categories.	Recall relevant information from experiences or gather relevant information from print and digital sources; take notes and categorize information, and provide a list of sources.	Recall relevant information from experiences or gather relevant information from print and digital sources; summarize or paraphrase information in notes and finished work, and provide a list of sources.

Demonstration

Anchor 8 calls for students to *gather information from print sources, digital sources, and experience* and to use it in a meaningful way to inform their writing. Successful information gathering usually begins with a question. Students read and reflect with a specific purpose in mind, and work to build information around a specified topic. They are systematic about gathering their information and systematic about what they read and document. In this way, competency with gathering information leads to focused learning and composing.

But think of students moving through a project and sorting through books, browsing the library, looking through websites, and rifling through the material you have available in the classroom—and having no specific purpose. When this is the case, good ideas often come to the surface but then get lost or forgotten in the shuffle. While browsing is acceptable in the early phases of a writing project, it does not accomplish what is needed to help students to gather key information that they can meaningfully use to inform their writing. At the elementary level, the Common Core State Standards call for students to locate specific information to answer questions, sort evidence into categories, take meaningful notes, integrate the information into the writing, and provide a list of sources.

Section 8 contains three versatile techniques/lessons for scaffolding these processes that can be used with K–5 students. The techniques are: *using note-taking forms, marking print sources,* and *marking digital sources.* With each technique, it is recommended that you demonstrate first, using the processes with a writing/research project of your own, and then support students as they use the approach independently or in groups. The lessons can serve as extensions to the research lessons presented in Section 7, or they can be connected with other content-area projects.

Using Note-Taking Forms

Using a form for note-taking, whether in relation to recalling information from experience or gathering information from print or digital sources, can help students to stay focused and on track as they prepare for and begin a writing project. Figures 8–1 and 8–2 offer generic forms that may be used or adapted for a variety of projects. Students write their specific question or topic at the top of the page and then record key information below. Before sending students off to work, demonstrate the process with your own question or topic, writing out or explaining the information you would include.

It is important to note that beginning in third grade, students are expected to sort their information into provided categories. By fourth grade, students are expected to begin categorizing on their own. Figure 8–2 provides support with categorizing. For example, students studying owls might be guided to use the form to take notes in relation to categories such as *physical characteristics*, *nesting*, *range*, and *diet*. Lots of early supported experiences working with categories will aid students in learning to identify and develop their own. Also note that by grade 4, students are expected to list the sources they have used, so Figure 8–2 includes a space that serves as a reminder.

When students are using information-gathering forms, sometimes just documenting the information—and talking about it—is enough. The process of reading and thinking through what to write down supports content-area learning, and that might be all you want to do. But other times, the collected information must be meaningfully integrated into a piece of writing. In this event it is important to show students how you make the transfer from notes to composition, and provide continued support as needed. The lessons in Section 7 make use of the forms as an integrated part of the research process.

Figure 8–1

Research Guide: K–2

Name: _____ Date: _____

Question or Topic

Information

Figure 8–2

Research Guide: Grades 3–5

Name: _____ Date: _____

Question or Topic

Category of Information

Information to Answer the Question
(You may use sticky notes here)

Category of Information

Information to Answer the Question
(You may use sticky notes here)

Figure 8–2 (*continued*)

Research Guide: Grades 3–5

**Category
of Information**

Information to Answer the Question
(You may use sticky notes here)

**Category
of Information**

Information to Answer the Question
(You may use sticky notes here)

**List of
Sources**

ANCHOR

8

Marking Print Sources

Marking is another useful tool for students to use as they are gathering information for a writing project. Marking involves organizing and annotating print-based materials so they can be easily retrieved and used to inform a piece of writing. Tools such as highlighting tape, highlighters, sticky notes, and book tabs work well for this process. They are used to mark pages or paragraphs, highlight key sections or words, and take brief notes at relevant places in the text.

Demonstrate the process with your own projects before asking students to mark on their own. For example, if your students are learning about birds, you might show them how to use a book tab to mark one section of an informational picture book as showing what birds eat and another as showing nesting habits. Then you might show how to use highlighting tape to mark key ideas or key words or phrases you want to return to. The goal of demonstrating the marking process is to show students the measures they can take to efficiently gather needed information from sources.

As students move into *categorizing* information (as required beginning in grade 3), they may need to take measures beyond basic marking. Having different *colors* of highlighting tape, highlighters, sticky notes, or book tabs on hand can be helpful. For example, in researching an influential figure in history, students might use yellow to code information about *demographics*, green for information about *childhood*, pink for *big accomplishments*, and blue for *impact on others*. Or rather than color coding, students can code with *words*, using a sticky note or scrap of paper to mark the area and writing in the relevant category (such as *childhood* or *accomplishments*).

Marking Digital Sources

With twenty-first-century literacy in mind, gathering and marking information from digital sources is just as important as working with print sources. Digital sources present a unique marking challenge, unless of course the material can be printed. *Printing* is one acceptable option.

But students need to learn to negotiate material as it is presented in an online environment, and there are tools and practices available for supporting this process.

In particular, *bookmarking sites* or *apps* can be useful for students working to gather and organize information. For example, Pearltrees (pearltrees.com) allows users to organize links to articles and other information in a web format. The program can be used on the Internet or downloaded as an app. You (the teacher) can create the web and allow students to search within, or you can demonstrate the process so that students or groups can create their own webs.

Diigo (diigo.com) is another bookmarking site that allows students to locate key pieces on the web and bookmark them for easy retrieval at a later time. The site allows for collecting, organizing, and sharing information from different web pages, and for students to electronically highlight text, create sticky notes summarizing key information, and tag and code specific pieces of information for later use. Apps and sites are being rapidly developed, so keep your eye out for tools that would work well in your setting.

Twenty-first-century literacy requires that students gain skill working with digital text, which remains uncharted territory in many elementary classrooms. Start small. You can start by choosing the search engine and suggesting the search terms. Or you can choose the website and even the web page. You can print pages at first to show students how to mark the material. You can show them how to save and store material, one document at a time, and how to use electronic highlighting and digital sticky notes, one tool at a time. But when your students master one skill, move to the next and keep them challenged. Monitor continually to ensure that quality searching, reading, and note taking are taking place, backing up to provide support as new challenges are encountered.

Independent Application

Information-gathering skills can be useful across the independent applications described in Sections 1–3. Figure 8–3 shows the genres that connect directly with information gathering.

Figure 8–3

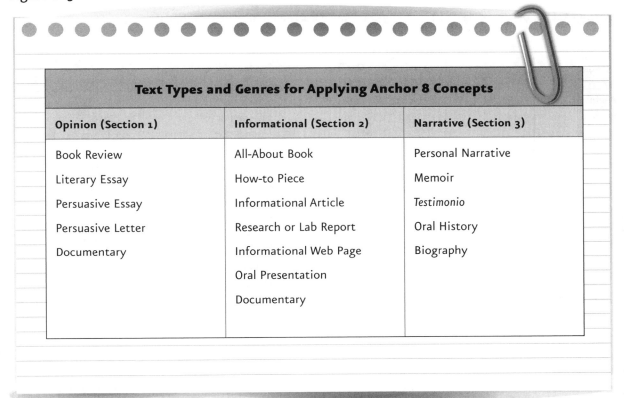

Text Types and Genres for Applying Anchor 8 Concepts		
Opinion (Section 1)	**Informational (Section 2)**	**Narrative (Section 3)**
Book Review	All-About Book	Personal Narrative
Literary Essay	How-to Piece	Memoir
Persuasive Essay	Informational Article	*Testimonio*
Persuasive Letter	Research or Lab Report	Oral History
Documentary	Informational Web Page	Biography
	Oral Presentation	
	Documentary	

RESEARCH TO BUILD AND PRESENT KNOWLEDGE

ANCHOR 9

English Language Arts Standards: Writing **ANCHOR 9**					
Writing Anchor 9: Draw evidence from literary or informational texts to support analysis, reflection, and research.					
Kindergarten	**First**	**Second**	**Third**	**Fourth**	**Fifth**
Begins in grade 4.	Begins in grade 4.	Begins in grade 4.	Begins in grade 4.	Draw evidence from literary or informational texts to support analysis, reflection, and research. **a.** Apply grade 4 Reading standards to literature (e.g., "Describe in depth a character, setting, or event in a story or drama, drawing on specific details in the text [e.g., a character's thoughts, words, or actions]"). **b.** Apply grade 4 Reading standards to informational texts (e.g., "Explain how an author uses reasons and evidence to support particular points in a text").	Draw evidence from literary or informational texts to support analysis, reflection, and research. **a.** Apply grade 5 Reading standards to literature (e.g., "Compare and contrast two or more characters, settings, or events in a story or a drama, drawing on specific details in the text [e.g., how characters interact]"). **b.** Apply grade 5 Reading standards to informational texts (e.g., "Explain how an author uses reasons and evidence to support particular points in a text, identifying which reasons and evidence support which point[s]").

Although the Common Core State Standards do not list specific expectations for Anchor 9 until grade 4, K–3 teachers should consider the lessons in this section, as they provide building blocks for the work of students in grades 4–5. Work toward Anchor 9 is relevant for students in all grades.

Demonstration

Anchor 9 calls for students to *draw evidence from literary or informational texts to support analysis, reflection, and research*. On any given day, student writers may have a variety of reasons for drawing evidence from text. They may be evaluating a piece of literature for the purpose of discussion or review; building an argument for a persuasive piece; working to critique the argument of another author; or reading to inform a research project.

When students *draw evidence* from text, they are expected to go beyond describing the information at a cursory level or simply repeating what the author has written. Instead, they are to analyze the material, reflect on it, and use it in insightful ways. We work extensively with these practices in the elementary grades because they are deeply facilitative of learning from texts, because they inspire rich conversations that extend knowledge, and because such practices give students power and depth in their writing.

In the interest of supporting students in drawing evidence from text, an overarching lesson is suggested, followed by options for continued exploration through collaborative engagement.

Overarching Lesson

To prepare for this lesson, be ready to demonstrate writing within a text type you have already taught (see Sections 1–3). Your choice should reflect an upcoming or current project or writing assignment. Your explicit focus will be on drawing evidence from text to support your writing.

1. **Purpose.** Tell students that using information or drawing evidence from other authors can strengthen their own writing. Let them know that you will be showing them how you think about this process in relation to your own work.

2. **Expectations.** Tell students that after your demonstration they will be considering the concepts you are discussing in light of their current pieces or their upcoming projects.

3. **Demonstration.**

   * Working with a draft you already have going, start the demonstration by stating your purpose for drawing evidence. For example, "I am showing the different ways we take care of our bodies," "I am working to make the case that English-only is not best for our community," "I want to find out if the robins at our feeder could be the same ones that were here last spring," or "I am arguing that this story has a 'never give up' theme."

   * Show students how you draw evidence from one or more texts and cite it in your writing. Some typical guiding questions you might address:

     * What information from this source will help me develop my point?

     * What details or examples should I include?

     Note: At this point in the lesson, you may wish to introduce an *evidence* form. See Figures 9–1 to 9–5 for examples. While these forms will provide a good starting point, it is recommended that you develop your own forms along the way to meet your students' particular needs within the genres you are teaching.

4. **Student Writing.** As students move to their writing and reading, encourage attention to the guiding questions you demonstrated in step 3.

5. **Assessment.** Let students know that you will be using their work to inform your next steps in instruction. Keep an eye out for your students to do the following, and plan your follow-up instruction accordingly:

   • Cite evidence to support opinions or key ideas.

   • Describe the evidence using appropriate detail.

   • Integrate and compare evidence across sources.

Figure 9–1

Gather Supporting Evidence from Informational Text

Name: _____ Date: _____

My Key Point or Opinion

Supporting details, examples, or pieces of information. (Use sticky notes or write in the space below.)

-
-
-

Sources

Figure 9–2

Integrate Information Across Texts

Name: _____ Date: _____

Jot down the evidence you are going to use from each text using sticky notes or the space below. You can draw straight lines to show points that are related. Use zigzag lines to show opposing or different views. List the authors or websites at the bottom.

My Key Point or Opinion

Important Points from Title 1

Important Points from Title 2

Source

Source

Figure 9–3

Gather Evidence for Analysis of Characters, Events, or Themes

Name: _____ Date: _____

Title: _____

An opinion
or observation about a
character, event,
or theme

Evidence from the text that supports your opinion or observation

-
-
-
-

Figure 9–4

ANCHOR

9

Character Analysis Web

Name: _____ Date: _____

Title: _____

Description of Character

Major Challenge or Goal

Character

Responses to Challenge/Goal

Character Changes over Time

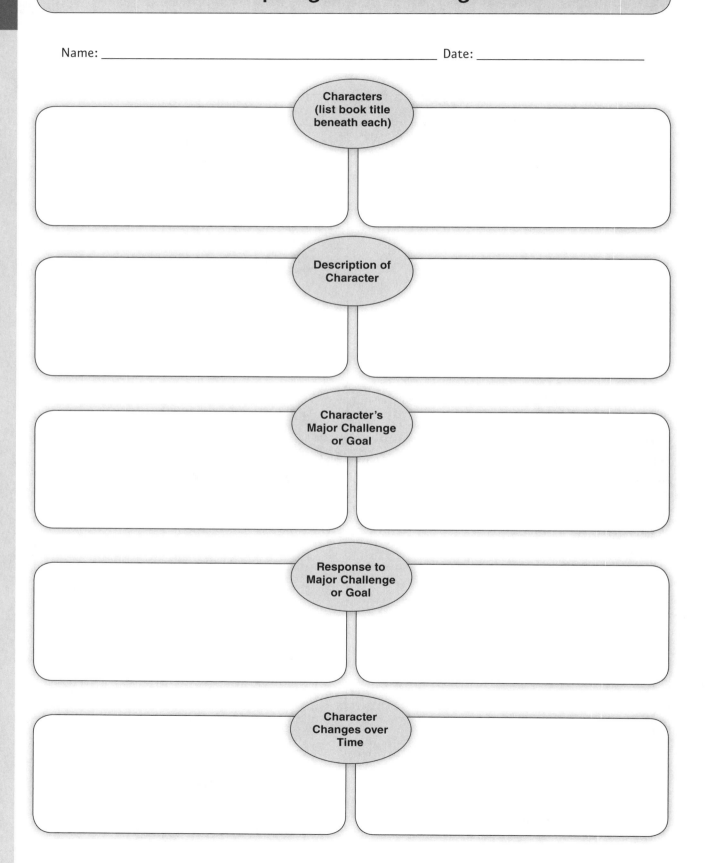

Chart for Comparing and Contrasting Characters

Figure 9–5

Name: _____ Date: _____

Characters (list book title beneath each)

Description of Character

Character's Major Challenge or Goal

Response to Major Challenge or Goal

Character Changes over Time

Collaborative Engagement

Analyze and Evaluate Writing Samples from the Classroom

After teaching students about drawing evidence from text and incorporating it into their writing, give groups a sample of student writing (or use teacher writing if you don't yet have a student sample) and show them how to analyze it in light of the reasoning or evidence used. You may wish to use questions such as those featured in Figure 9–6. If several groups are working on this project, arrange time for the groups to report their findings and observations.

Conferring with the Teacher

Because the nature of using evidence from text varies across pieces and depends on the skill of the reader, individualized conferences are an important part of the instructional process for Anchor 9. When students are using text-based evidence in their writing, have them bring their source material to the conference so you can check in with them and see how they are integrating the content. Organizing the conference with a predictable set of prompts and questions can help students know what to expect and be ready to show you their thinking. See Figure 9–7.

Conferring with Peers

Children can be very capable and responsible responders to their peers' writing, especially when they are given some starting expectations for their conversations. After they have some experience conferring with you, coach them to work in peer conferences or small groups through one of the processes featured in Figure 9–8.

Figure 9–6

Questions for Analyzing and Evaluating the Use of Evidence (for Grades 3–5)

- What reasoning or evidence from the text is used to back up/inform key opinions and ideas?
- What examples or details were used?
- Does any evidence or information seem missing?

Figure 9–7

Conference Routine

- **Open the conversation**. *How are things going with this piece? Tell me about it/ read this part to me. How are you doing with drawing evidence from sources?*

- **Identify notable strengths.** *Here is a good example of using evidence from the text to back up your opinion. . . . This is just what you need to support your point.*

- **Identify one teaching point.** *What do you think you should work on from here? Can you show me how you will start? Or There is one part I want you to develop and I'm going to help you get started.*

- **Send the student away with something manageable to develop.** *Let's get you started on this and then next time we meet we can talk about how it's going.*

Figure 9–8

Peer Conference Plans

- Ask the author to tell you his or her key points or ideas and show you the evidence or examples he or she has built for each. If evidence or examples are not used at key points, help the author get started.

- Look together for places the author has drawn evidence from text and mark them with a book tab. Discuss the parts. Is there anything that could be developed or clarified?

Independent Application

Drawing evidence from text is a skill that can be useful across the independent applications described in Sections 1–3. Figure 9–9 shows the genres that make particular use of this skill.

Figure 9–9

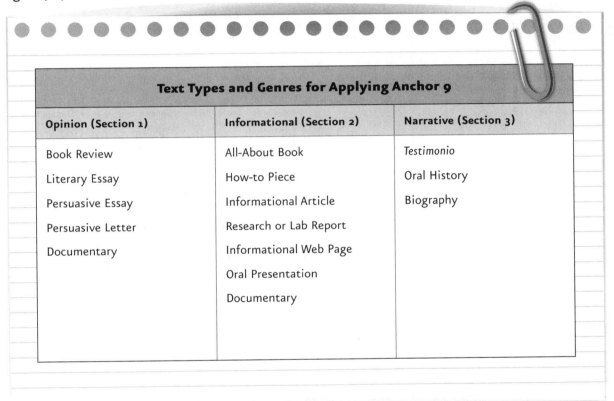

Text Types and Genres for Applying Anchor 9		
Opinion (Section 1)	**Informational (Section 2)**	**Narrative (Section 3)**
Book Review	All-About Book	*Testimonio*
Literary Essay	How-to Piece	Oral History
Persuasive Essay	Informational Article	Biography
Persuasive Letter	Research or Lab Report	
Documentary	Informational Web Page	
	Oral Presentation	
	Documentary	

RANGE OF WRITING

ANCHOR 10

English Language Arts Standards: Writing ANCHOR 10

Writing Anchor 10: Write routinely over extended time frames (time for research, reflection, and revision) and shorter time frames (a single sitting or a day or two) for a range of discipline-specific tasks, purposes, and audiences.

Kindergarten	First	Second	Third	Fourth	Fifth
Begins in grade 3.	Begins in grade 3.	Begins in grade 3.	Write routinely over extended time frames (time for research, reflection, and revision) and shorter time frames (a single sitting or a day or two) for a range of discipline-specific tasks, purposes, and audiences.	Write routinely over extended time frames (time for research, reflection, and revision) and shorter time frames (a single sitting or a day or two) for a range of discipline-specific tasks, purposes, and audiences.	Write routinely over extended time frames (time for research, reflection, and revision) and shorter time frames (a single sitting or a day or two) for a range of discipline-specific tasks, purposes, and audiences.

Although the Common Core document does not list specific expectations for Anchor 10 until grade 3, K–2 teachers should make an effort toward these expectations, as they provide building blocks for the work that will eventually be required of students in grades 3–5. Working toward Anchor 10 is relevant for students in all grades.

Supporting Routine and Wide Writing

Anchor 10 is an all-encompassing standard that serves as an umbrella for the other nine. The goal is that students will *write routinely over extended time frames (time for research, reflection, and revision) and shorter time frames (a single sitting or a day or two) for a range of discipline-specific tasks, purposes, and audiences.* While this standard officially begins in grade 3, we start the effort in kindergarten and continue it through the grades by offering a range of writing experiences in a range of settings, and working with a range of genres as described in Sections 1–3.

The ultimate goal in having K–5 students write routinely and for a variety of reasons is of course not simply to prepare them for tests; nor is it really even to render them college- and career-ready—though both of these goals will be nurtured along the way. The ultimate goal is to enable students to effectively use writing for an ever-increasing range of tasks, purposes, and audiences *in ways that are meaningful to their lives today.* Writing is important for the test, and it's important for college and career, but it is much more important for other things when children are six or eight or ten years old.

In the daily life of an elementary student, writing can be used to connect with others, to entertain, to persuade, and to inform. It can be used to establish identity, to make an impact on others' thinking or way of doing things, and to help make sense of the world. Elementary students don't become motivated to write as they think about far-in-the-future tests or about the high school or college experience. They become motivated to write when writing serves a function in their everyday lives. If we want elementary students to write routinely—and to do it with the motivation and engagement that propel continued learning—we have to keep writing meaningful in light of whom they are today.

Class Record for Opinion Writing: Kindergarten

Student Names	Grade-Level Expectations			
	Tells the topic or title.		States opinion or preference.	
	Date	Date	Date	Date

0 = Not Present   **1 = Could Use Development**   **2 = Developed**

Class Record for Informative/Explanatory Writing: Kindergarten

Student Names	Grade-Level Expectations			
	Names the topic.		Supplies some information about the topic.	
	Date	Date	Date	Date

0 = Not Present   **1 = Could Use Development**   **2 = Developed**

Class Record for Narrative Writing: Kindergarten

Student Names	Grade-Level Expectations			
	Tells about an event or linked events in the order in which they occurred.		Reacts to what happened.	
	Date	Date	Date	Date

0 = Not Present   **1 = Could Use Development**   **2 = Developed**

K–5 Class Record for Language Conventions (Language Standard 2)*

Grade Level: _____

Student Names	Grade-Level Expectations					
	Capitals		Punctuation		Spelling	
	Date	Date	Date	Date	Date	Date

0 = Not Present　　　　**1 = Could Use Development**　　　　**2 = Developed**

*See Figure 5–3 or Common Core Language Standard 2 for specific grade-level expectations.

Class Record for Opinion Writing: Grade 1

Student Names	Grade-Level Expectations							
	Introduces the topic or title.		States an opinion.		Supplies a reason for the opinion.		Provides a sense of closure.	
	Date	Date	Date	Date	Date	Date	Date	Date

0 = Not Present   1 = Could Use Development   2 = Developed

Class Record for Informative/Explanatory Writing: Grade 1

Student Names	Grade-Level Expectations					
	Names the topic.		Supplies some facts about the topic.		Provides closure.	
	Date	Date	Date	Date	Date	Date

0 = Not Present   **1 = Could Use Development**   **2 = Developed**

Class Record for Narrative Writing: Grade 1

Student Names	Grade-Level Expectations							
	Recounts two or more appropriately sequenced events.		Includes details about what happened.		Uses words to signal event order.		Provides closure.	
	Date	Date	Date	Date	Date	Date	Date	Date

0 = Not Present   **1 = Could Use Development**   **2 = Developed**

Class Record for Opinion Writing: Grade 2

Student Names	Grade-Level Expectations									
	Introduces the topic or text.		States an opinion.		Supplies reasons that support the opinion.		Uses linking words.		Provides a conclusion.	
	Date	Date	Date	Date	Date	Date	Date	Date	Date	Date

0 = Not Present   1 = Could Use Development   2 = Developed

Class Record for Informative/Explanatory Writing: Grade 2

Student Names	Grade-Level Expectations					
	Introduces the topic.		Uses facts and definitions to develop points.		Provides a conclusion.	
	Date	Date	Date	Date	Date	Date

0 = Not Present   1 = Could Use Development   2 = Developed

Class Record for Narrative Writing: Grade 2

Student Names	Grade-Level Expectations							
	Recounts an elaborated event or short sequence of events.		Includes details to describe actions, thoughts, and feelings.		Uses words to signal event order.		Provides closure.	
	Date	Date	Date	Date	Date	Date	Date	Date

0 = Not Present   1 = Could Use Development   2 = Developed

Class Record for Opinion Writing: Grade 3

Student Names	Grade-Level Expectations											
	Introduces the topic or text.		States an opinion.		Creates a structure that lists reasons.		Provides reasons that support the opinion.		Uses linking words and phrases.		Provides a conclusion.	
	Date	Date	Date	Date	Date	Date	Date	Date	Date	Date	Date	Date

0 = Not Present   1 = Could Use Development   2 = Developed

Class Record for Informative/Explanatory Writing: Grade 3

Student Names	Grade-Level Expectations							
	Introduces the topic. Groups related information together. Includes illustrations as useful.		Develops the topic with facts, definitions, and details.		Uses linking words and phrases.		Provides a conclusion.	
	Date	Date	Date	Date	Date	Date	Date	Date

0 = Not Present   1 = Could Use Development   2 = Developed

Class Record for Narrative Writing: Grade 3

Student Names	Grade-Level Expectations							
	Establishes a situation and narrator and/or characters; organizes an event sequence.		Uses dialogue and descriptions of actions, thoughts, and feelings to develop experiences and events or show character views.		Uses words and phrases to signal event order.		Provides closure.	
	Date	Date	Date	Date	Date	Date	Date	Date

0 = Not Present　　　　**1 = Could Use Development**　　　　**2 = Developed**

Class Record for Anchor 4: Grades 3–5

Student Names	Grade-Level Expectations					
	Writing is clear and coherent.		Content and format are appropriate to task, purpose, and audience.		Voice and style are appropriate to task, purpose, and audience.	
	Date	Date	Date	Date	Date	Date

0 = Not Present   1 = Could Use Development   2 = Developed

Class Record for Opinion Writing: Grade 4

Student Names	Grade-Level Expectations											
	Introduces the topic or text.		States an opinion.		Creates a structure for grouping related ideas.		Provides reasons supported by facts and details.		Uses linking words and phrases.		Provides a conclusion related to the opinion.	
	Date	Date	Date	Date	Date	Date	Date	Date	Date	Date	Date	Date

0 = Not Present   **1 = Could Use Development**   **2 = Developed**

Class Record for Informative/Explanatory Writing: Grade 4

Student Names	Grade-Level Expectations									
	Introduces the topic. Groups related information by paragraphs and sections. Includes formatting, illustrations, and multimedia as useful.		Develops the topic with facts, definitions, details, quotations, or other information and examples.		Links ideas within categories of information.		Uses precise language and domain-specific vocabulary.		Provides a conclusion.	
	Date	Date	Date	Date	Date	Date	Date	Date	Date	Date

0 = Not Present   1 = Could Use Development   2 = Developed

Class Record for Narrative Writing: Grade 4

Student Names	Grade-Level Expectations									
	Establishes a situation and introduces a narrator and/or characters; organizes an event sequence.		Uses dialogue and description to develop events or show responses of characters.		Uses a variety of words and phrases to manage the event sequence.		Uses concrete words and phrases and sensory details.		Provides a conclusion that follows from the narrated events.	
	Date	Date	Date	Date	Date	Date	Date	Date	Date	Date

0 = Not Present   1 = Could Use Development   2 = Developed

© 2013 by Gretchen Owocki, from *The Common Core Writing Book, K–5*. Portsmouth, NH: Heinemann.

Class Record for Opinion Writing: Grade 5

Student Names	Grade-Level Expectations											
	Introduces the topic or text.		States an opinion.		Creates a structure that logically groups ideas.		Provides logically ordered reasons supported by facts and details.		Uses linking words, phrases, and clauses.		Provides a conclusion related to the opinion.	
	Date	Date	Date	Date	Date	Date	Date	Date	Date	Date	Date	Date

0 = Not Present   1 = Could Use Development   2 = Developed

Class Record for Informative/Explanatory Writing: Grade 5

Student Names	Grade-Level Expectations									
	Introduces the topic. Provides a general observation and focus, grouping related information logically. Includes formatting, illustrations, and multimedia as useful.		Develops the topic with facts, definitions, details, quotations, or other information and examples.		Links ideas within categories of information.		Uses precise language and domain-specific vocabulary.		Provides a conclusion.	
	Date	Date	Date	Date	Date	Date	Date	Date	Date	Date

0 = Not Present   **1 = Could Use Development**   **2 = Developed**

Class Record for Narrative Writing: Grade 5

Student Names	Grade-Level Expectations									
	Establishes a situation and introduces a narrator and/or characters; organizes an event sequence.		Uses dialogue, description, and pacing to develop events or show responses of characters.		Uses a variety of words, phrases, and clauses to manage the event sequence.		Uses concrete words and phrases and sensory details.		Provides a conclusion that follows from the narrated events.	
	Date	Date	Date	Date	Date	Date	Date	Date	Date	Date

0 = Not Present   1 = Could Use Development   2 = Developed

Works Cited

Adler, R. 1989. *Writing Together: A Peer-Editing Approach to Composition.* Dubuque, IA: Kendall-Hunt.

Calkins, L., M. Ehrenworth, and C. Lehman. 2012. *Pathways to the Common Core: Accelerating Achievement.* Portsmouth, NH: Heinemann.

Culham, R. 2003. *6 + 1 Traits of Writing: The Complete Guide Grades 3 and Up.* New York: Scholastic.

———. 2005. *6 + 1 Traits of Writing: Primary Grades.* New York: Scholastic.

Cunningham, P., and R. Allington. 2011. *Classrooms That Work: They Can All Read and Write.* Boston: Allyn & Bacon.

Graham, S. 2008. *The Power of Word Processing for the Student Writer.* Wisconsin Rapids, WI: Renaissance Learning.

Graves, D. 1983. *Writing: Teachers and Children at Work.* Portsmouth, NH: Heinemann.

Owocki, G. 2012. *The Common Core Lesson Book, K–5: Working with Increasingly Complex Literature, Informational Text, and Foundational Reading Skills.* Portsmouth, NH: Heinemann.

Saavedra, C. 2011. "Language and Literacy in the Borderlands: Acting Upon the World Through Testimonios." *Language Arts* 88 (4): 261–69.

Writing Now. 2008. *Writing Now: A Policy Research Brief Produced by the National Council of Teachers of English.* Available at www.ncte.org/library/NCTEFiles/Resources/PolicyResearch/WrtgResearchBrief.pdf.